ArcGIS 9

What is ArcGIS 9.2?

Contents

1 GIS concepts and requirements

"GIS is evolving from a database approach to a knowledge approach."

ESRI President Jack Dangermond

Geography has traditionally provided an important framework and language for organizing and communicating key concepts about the world.

Knowledge is shared through many abstract forms. Attempts to articulate and explain human experience and understanding use these abstractions—summaries of a larger body of knowledge. Abstractions, such as text, hieroglyphics, language, mathematics and statistics, music and art, drawings, images, and maps, are used to record and communicate experiences, culture, and history from generation to generation.

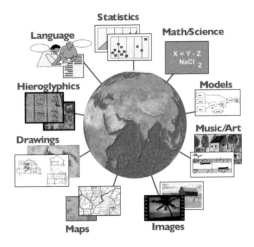

Many abstractions are used to communicate the understanding of the earth and its systems. Geography provides a universal framework for abstraction and communication of "place".

Digital computing allows the capture and sharing of knowledge across networks such as the Internet. Simultaneously, geographic information system (GIS) technology is evolving and provides a critical methodology to understand, represent, manage, and communicate the many aspects of physical and human landscapes—and to better understand the earth as a system.

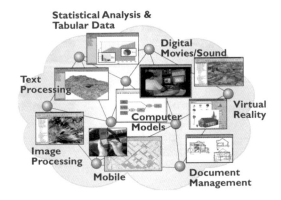

Digital technology is increasingly used to capture, share, and store knowledge.

FIVE ELEMENTS OF GEOGRAPHIC KNOWLEDGE

A GIS is a system for the management, analysis, and display of geographic knowledge, which is represented using a series of information sets. GIS abstracts geographic knowledge into five basic elements:

- Geographic datasets and data models

- Maps and globes

- Geoprocessing models and scripts

- GIS methods and workflows

- Metadata

These five information sets are the primary elements of geographic information.

Geographic datasets and data models

Geographic datasets are spatially-referenced observations, measurements, features, descriptions, images, tabular data, surveys, and so on that describe geography. Data models are used to organize geographic information in files and databases, containing geographic information elements—for example, features, rasters, and their descriptive attributes.

Data models embody classification systems, semantic definitions, rules, and relationships that describe rich geographic behavior required in each application.

GIS datasets require more than database management system (DBMS) tables or individual data files on disk. Geodatabases incorporate rich behavior and integrity rules. Data models play a critical role in GIS by defining the schema, behavior, and integrity rules in each system.

Maps and globes

Maps and globes contain interactive views of geographic data with which to answer questions and communicate results. They provide the advanced GIS applications for interacting with geographic data. Maps are cartographic representations and computer visualizations of geography used to represent and communicate geographic phenomena. Maps and globes leverage computer graphic techniques to render scientific and cultural data. These documents enable cartographic knowledge to be more consistently communicated and widely shared.

Geoprocessing models and scripts

Geoprocessing is the methodical execution of a sequence of operations on geographic data to create new information—for example, to create sophisticated analytical models and automate GIS tasks. Geoprocessing provides the ability for users to program their ideas and concepts as well as to automate work and be more productive.

GIS methods and workflows

GIS tasks are based on a series of methods and best practices—map generation, data editing, analysis and modeling, visualization, and information management. A key aspect of successful GIS use is the development and application of a series of workflows and procedures. Workflows that are unique to GIS require the application of best practices to effectively leverage the full potential of GIS.

Metadata

Metadata documents describe other elements of geographic information. A metadata catalog enables users to organize, discover, and gain access to shared geographic knowledge.

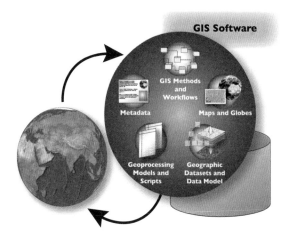

GIS abstracts geography into five basic elements used for representing geographic knowledge. These elements, along with advanced software, provide the building blocks for Intelligent GIS.

These elements of geographic knowledge, along with comprehensive software logic, form the building blocks for assembling an intelligent GIS.

Intelligent GIS makes it possible for users to digitally encapsulate and share geographic knowledge. These elements provide a foundation for addressing many challenges using GIS—for example, improving efficiency, making informed decisions, applying science-based planning methods, and performing resource accounting.

GIS enables users to capture and share geographic knowledge in many forms such as advanced GIS datasets, maps, data models, standardized workflows, and advanced models of geographic processes. Intelligent GIS also enables the building and management of central GIS servers that can be used to serve and share these five elements of geographic information and applications across organizations.

GIS software must be engineered to enable the creation, use, management, and sharing of all five elements of geographic information.

Many have characterized GIS as one of the most powerful of all information technologies because it focuses on integrating knowledge from multiple sources and creates a crosscutting environment for collaboration.

In addition, GIS is attractive to most people who encounter it because it is both intuitive and cognitive. It combines a powerful visualization environment with a strong analytic and modeling framework that is rooted in the science of geography.

This combination has resulted in a technology that is science-based, trusted, and easily communicated across cultures, social classes, languages, and disciplines.

To support this vision, a GIS needs to support several views for working with geographic information:

1. The geodatabase view: A GIS is a spatial database containing datasets that represent geographic information in terms of a generic GIS data model— features, rasters, attributes, topologies, networks, and so forth.

2. The geovisualization view: A GIS is a set of intelligent maps and other views that show features and feature relationships on the earth's surface. Various map views of the underlying geographic information can be constructed and used as "windows into the geographic database" to support query, analysis, and editing of geographic information. Each GIS has a series of two-dimensional (2D) and three-dimensional (3D) map applications that provide rich tools for working with geographic information through these views.

3. The geoprocessing view: A GIS is a set of information transformation tools that derive new information from existing datasets. These geoprocessing functions take information from existing datasets, apply analytic functions, and write results into new derived datasets. Geoprocessing involves the ability to program your work and to automate workflows by assembling an ordered sequence of operations.

These three GIS views are represented in ESRI® ArcGIS® by the catalog and the geodatabase (a GIS is a collection of geographic datasets), the map (a GIS is an intelligent map view), and the toolbox (a GIS is a set of geoprocessing tools). Together, all three are critical parts of a complete GIS and are used at varying levels in all GIS applications.

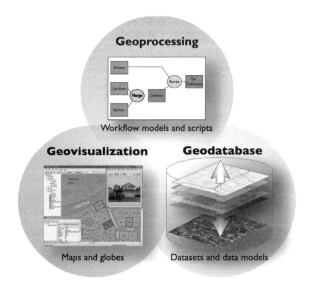

Three views of a GIS for working with key elements of geographic information. All elements can be described, documented, and shared through metadata.

Geographic datasets can represent:

- Raw measurements such as satellite imagery

- Compiled and interpreted information such as soils polygons and parcel boundaries

- Data that is derived through geoprocessing operations for analysis and modeling

Here is a quick review of some key geodata principles that are important in GIS.

THEMATIC LAYERS AND DATASETS

In a GIS, homogeneous collections of geographic objects are organized into a series of data themes, or layers, that cover a given map extent—for example, roads, rivers, place names, buildings, parcels, political boundaries, surface elevation, and satellite imagery.

Many of the spatial relationships between layers can be easily derived through their common geographic location.

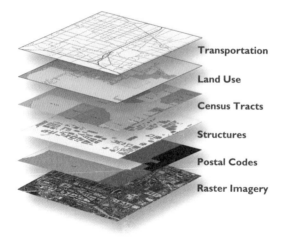

Transportation

Land Use

Census Tracts

Structures

Postal Codes

Raster Imagery

GIS integrates many types of spatial data.

Describing the correct location and shape of features requires a framework for defining real-world locations. A geographic coordinate system is used to assign geographic locations to objects. A global coordinate system of latitude-longitude is one such framework. Another is a planar, or projected, coordinate system derived from the global framework.

TYPES OF GEOGRAPHIC DATASETS

ArcGIS manages simple data layers as generic GIS object classes and utilizes a rich collection of tools to work with the data layers to derive many key relationships.

A key geographic data concept is the dataset. It is the primary mechanism used to organize and apply geographic information in ArcGIS. A GIS contains three primary dataset types:

- **Feature classes.** Ordered collections of vector-based features (for example, sets of points, lines, and polygons).

- **Raster datasets** such as digital elevation models and imagery.

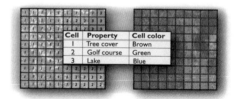

Cell	Property	Cell color
1	Tree cover	Brown
2	Golf course	Green
3	Lake	Blue

- **Associated attribute tables** containing descriptive information about geographic objects and features.

GIS DATA TYPES

Users typically start by building a number of these fundamental dataset types. As part of a GIS geodatabase design, users specify how certain features will be represented. For example, parcels will typically be represented as polygons, streets will be mapped as centerlines, wells as points, and so on.

Once feature representations are organized into datasets (that is, as feature classes, raster datasets, and tables), then users add to or extend their geodatabase with more advanced capabilities.

Users add a rich set of geodatabase data types such as topologies, networks, and subtypes to model GIS behavior, to maintain data integrity, and to work with an important set of spatial relationships.

Examples of extended GIS data types include:

- **Networks** that are used to connect individual features in transportation, water, facilities, and other networks.

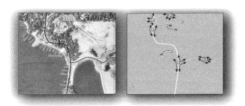

- **Terrains** and digital elevation models (DEMs) that are used to model surface elevation and other three-dimensional surfaces.

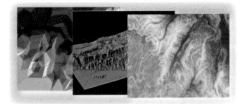

- **Coordinate Geometry (COGO) and survey measurements** to provide the control framework for high precision GIS datasets.

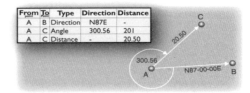

From	To	Type	Direction	Distance
A	B	Direction	N87E	-
A	C	Angle	300.56	201
A	C	Distance	-	20.50

- **Other data types**, such as address and place name locators, linear referencing systems, cadastral fabrics for parcel management, and cartographic representations.

Addresses
3350 45th Ave NE
3383 30th Ave NE
2459 Country Rd. 9 NE

Address Locator

DESCRIPTIVE ATTRIBUTES

Attribute tables and relationships play a key role in GIS data models, just as they do in traditional database applications. GIS datasets include traditional tabular attributes in addition to their geographic representations.

Attributes are used to describe geographic objects such as features and rasters. Many tables can be linked to the geographic features using a common field, or key.

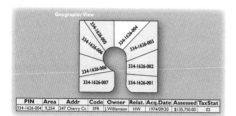

GIS DATASETS ARE SHARED ACROSS ORGANIZATIONS

A GIS will use numerous datasets with many representations, often from many organizations. Therefore, it is important for GIS datasets to be:

- Simple to use and easy to understand

- Used easily with other geographic datasets

- Effectively compiled and validated

- Clearly documented for content, intended uses, and purposes

Any GIS database or file base will adhere to these common principles and concepts. Each GIS requires a mechanism for describing geographic data in these terms, along with a comprehensive set of tools to use and manage this information.

Maps provide a powerful metaphor to define and standardize how people use and interact with geographic information. Interactive maps provide the primary user interface for most GIS applications. Users can point to locations and discover new relationships, perform editing and analysis, and effectively communicate results using geographic views such as maps and globes.

Interactive maps, printed maps, 3D scenes and globes, summary charts and tables, time-based views, and schematic views of networks are examples of how GIS users view and interact with geographic information.

ArcMap™ is the primary application in ArcGIS for creating and interacting with maps. With the ArcGIS 3D Analyst™ extension, 3D global views can be created and used in ArcGlobe™.

GIS maps provide access to geographic information and include a range of tools for working with and interacting with the map contents.

Developers often embed maps in custom applications, and many users publish Web maps on the Internet for focused GIS use.

Map layers are used to assign symbols and to label features based on feature attribute values. For example, parcels can be shaded with colors based on their zoning types, or the size of point symbols for oil wells can be specified based on production levels. The oil wells could also be labeled with ownership information.

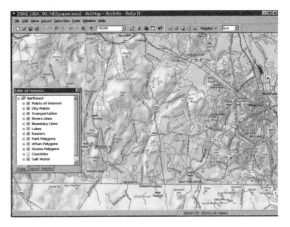

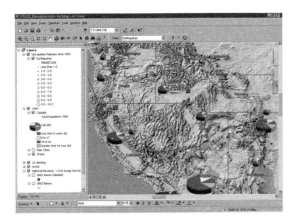

GIS users pan and zoom to navigate around an interactive map. Using an interactive GIS map, users can point to a geographic object to get information about the object. Spatial queries can be performed. For example, stores of a certain type can be found within a specified distance of schools; or the wetland areas within 500 meters of selected roads can be identified. In addition, GIS users can edit data and feature representations through interactive GIS maps.

Maps are used to communicate geographic information as well as to perform numerous tasks, including advanced data compilation, cartography, analysis, query, and field GIS use.

Through interactive GIS maps, users perform common GIS tasks from simple to advanced. It's the main "business form" in a GIS that enables access to geographic information for an organization.

In addition to traditional two-dimensional maps, other interactive views are used as views into GIS databases—for example, temporal views and animations, 3D globes, and schematic drawings.

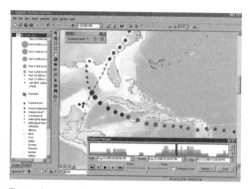

Temporal views used to track hurricanes

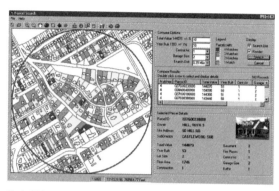

Embedded maps within custom applications

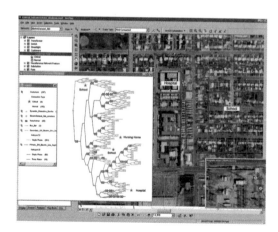

Schematics drawing used to display gas lines

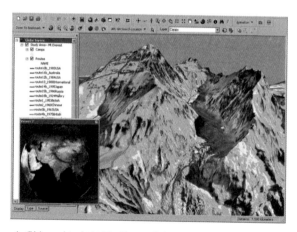

ArcGlobe used to depict Mt. Everest climbing routes

COMMON CHARACTERISTICS OF GIS MAPS

A GIS map is an interactive map that is accessed and used on a computer or a mobile device. GIS maps extend traditional printed maps in several ways:

- GIS maps are multiscale. They can automatically display information at the appropriate level of detail as you zoom in and out on the map—from a global view down to a street level or city-block view.

- GIS maps are interactive. You can often work with information ad hoc and add new layers of information as they become available.

- Each GIS map has a set of tools as part of its user interface that allow you to work with its contents. Capabilities can vary from common map query and identification tasks, to address geocoding, routing, data compilation and editing, and geographic analysis. Many maps contain focused, custom tools that help end users accomplish critical work tasks.

- GIS maps can be dynamic and animate the display of information through time.

- GIS maps come in many applications and map sizes and can be deployed as Web maps, 3D maps, specialized map applications, and mobile maps in the field.

- GIS maps often fuse information from a range of GIS Web services. The ability to integrate information and tools from multiple sources is quite powerful.

- GIS maps are flexible. A variety of GIS map applications and frameworks support a wide range of deployment options.

ArcGIS map types

Users work with many types of GIS maps to accomplish work tasks—for example, professional GIS maps, Web maps, embedded maps, explorer maps, and mobile maps.

Each map type has a corresponding GIS software application that is used to perform tasks. Each GIS map type is suitable for certain user audiences and workflows.

Professional GIS Maps

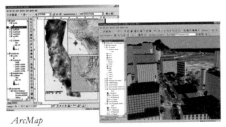

ArcMap

ArcGlobe

Embedded Maps

ArcGIS Engine

Web Maps

Web mapping application included with ArcGIS Server and ArcIMS®

Mobile Maps

ArcPad® and ArcGIS Mobile

2D and 3D Map Explorers

ArcGIS Explorer

Geoprocessing is the methodical execution of a sequence of operations on geographic data to create new information. The process you perform may be routine, for example, to help you convert a number of files from one format to another. Or the operations can be quite advanced—to create high quality maps, to create a sophisticated analytical model to help you understand and solve important scientific problems, and to build GIS modeling Web services.

The fundamental purpose of geoprocessing is to automate GIS tasks. Almost all uses of GIS involve the repetition of work, and this creates the need for methods to automate, document, and share multistep, repeatable procedures.

ArcGIS includes a rich set of tools to work with and process geographic information. This collection of tools is used to operate on GIS information objects, such as datasets, attribute fields, and cartographic elements for printed maps. Together, these comprehensive tools and the data objects on which they operate form the basis of a rich geoprocessing framework.

DATA + TOOL = NEW DATA

GIS tools are the building blocks for assembling multistep operations. A tool applies an operation to existing data to derive new data. The geoprocessing framework in ArcGIS is used to string together a series of these operations, enabling users to automate workflows, program analytical models, and build scripts to execute frequently used procedures.

Stringing a sequence of operations together forms a process model that is used to automate and record numerous geoprocessing tasks in the GIS. The building and application of such procedures is referred to as geoprocessing.

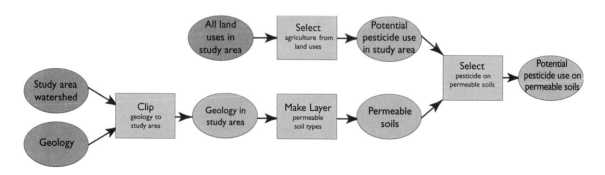

A complete GIS contains geographic datasets and a set of GIS operators to work with the information. ArcGIS has a rich GIS language with thousands of operators that work on all the various geographic data types in a GIS.

GEOPROCESSING IN ACTION

Geoprocessing is used in virtually all phases of a GIS for data automation and compilation, data management, analysis and modeling, and advanced cartography.

Geoprocessing is used to model how data flows from one structure to another to perform many common GIS tasks—for example, to import data from numerous formats, integrate that data into the GIS, and perform a number of standard quality validation checks against the imported data, as well as perform powerful analysis and modeling. The ability to automate and repeat such workflows is a key capability in a GIS. Geoprocessing is widely applied in numerous GIS applications and scenarios.

One method used to build geoprocessing workflows is to execute a number of tools in a specific sequence. Users can compose such processes graphically using the ModelBuilder™ application in ArcGIS, and they can compose scripts using modern scripting tools, such as Python®, VBScript™, and JavaScript®.

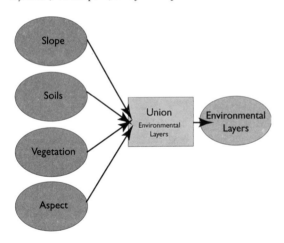

ArcGIS includes a set of tools and data types that can be assembled into processes in a geoprocessing framework. Many multistep geoprocessing operations can be authored, executed, and shared.

DATA COMPILATION

Data compilation procedures are automated using geoprocessing to ensure data quality and integrity and to perform repetitive quality assurance/quality control (QA/QC) tasks. Automating these workflows using geoprocessing helps share and communicate the series of procedures, perform batch processing flows, and document these key processes for derived data.

ANALYSIS AND MODELING

Geoprocessing is the key framework for modeling and analysis. Some common modeling applications include:

- Models for suitability and capability, prediction, and assessment of alternative scenarios

- Integration of external models

- Model sharing

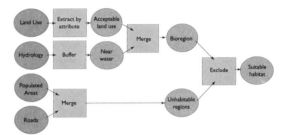

Models can be shared within an organization

DATA MANAGEMENT

Managing GIS data flows is critical in all GIS applications. GIS users apply geoprocessing functions to move data in and out of databases; publish data in many formats, such as in Geography Markup Language (GML) profiles; join adjacent datasets; update GIS database schemas; and perform batch processes on their GIS databases.

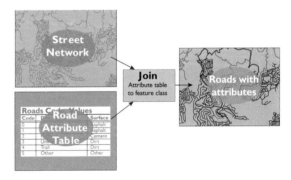

Creating new data by combining existing data

CARTOGRAPHY

Advanced geoprocessing tools are used to derive multiscale cartographic representations, perform generalization logic, and automate much of the cartographic QA/QC workflows for print-quality map products.

GIS information management shares many of the same concepts and characteristics with standard information technology (IT) architectures and can work well in centralized, enterprise computing environments. For example, GIS datasets can be managed in relational databases, just like other enterprise information. Advanced application logic is used to operate on the data stored in the DBMS. Like other transactional enterprise information, GIS systems are used to manage constant change and updates in geographic databases. However, some data update transactions in a GIS often differ in a number of critical aspects.

GIS DATA IS COMPLEX

GIS data volumes are quite large in the number and size of elements. For example, a simple database query to populate a common business form delivers a few rows of data from the DBMS, while a map draw in a GIS will require a database query that returns hundreds, even thousands of records. In addition, the vector or raster geometry being retrieved for display can be several megabytes and larger in size for each feature. GIS data also has complex relationships and structures, such as networks, terrains, and topologies.

GIS DATA COMPILATION IS AN ADVANCED, SPECIALIZED ACTIVITY

Comprehensive editing applications are required to graphically build and maintain GIS datasets. Specialized processing, along with geographic rules and commands, are necessary to maintain the integrity and behavior of geographic features and rasters. Hence, GIS data compilation can be challenging. This is one of the compelling reasons why users often share GIS datasets.

GIS INVOLVES A UNIQUE COMBINATION OF SCIENTIFIC AND BUSINESS COMPUTING

GIS users work with numerous datasets in many formats and data structures simultaneously. In addition to dataset compilation, users constantly produce new result sets and generate model results, maps, globes, layers, and reports. Many of these can be shared and used more than once, while other results are reserved for personal use.

A complete GIS includes management tools to organize and manage the information collections resulting from these workflows. In addition, the GIS must also provide a means for cataloging and sharing this information via metadata.

A GIS IS TRANSACTIONAL

As in other database management systems, numerous data updates are constantly being posted to a GIS database. Hence, GIS databases, like other databases, must support update transactions. However, GIS users have some specialized transactional requirements. The main concept underlying this is often referred to as a long transaction.

In a GIS, a single editing operation can involve changes to multiple rows in multiple tables. Users need to be able to undo and redo their changes before they are committed. Editing sessions can span a few hours or even days. Often the edits must be performed in a system that is disconnected from the central, shared database.

In many cases, database updates pass through a series of phases. For example, within the utilities industry, common work stages include working, proposed, accepted, under construction, and as built. The process is essentially cyclical. The work order is initially generated, assigned to an engineer, and modified over time as it progresses from stage to stage; finally, the changes are committed, or applied back to the corporate database.

GIS workflow processes may span days and months. Yet the GIS database still requires continuous availability for daily operations where users might have their own views or states of the shared GIS database.

Often, users want to synchronize GIS data contents among a series of database copies, called replicas, where each site performs its own updates on its local database.

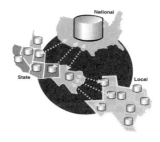

Periodically, the users want to transfer the updates from each database replica to the others and synchronize their contents. Many times, the DBMSs are different—for example, users want to replicate and synchronize data across a range of commercial DBMSs such as SQL Server, Oracle®, and IBM® DB2®.

Today, there is widespread recognition that the data layers and tables in most geographic information systems come from multiple organizations. Each GIS organization develops some, but not all, of its data content. At least some of the layers come from outside the organization.

The need for data drives users to acquire their data in the most effective and timely manner, including acquiring portions of their GIS databases from other GIS users.

In addition, users are increasingly publishing, accessing, and integrating geographic information using Web services.

GIS management is distributed among many departments and across organizations.

INTEROPERABILITY

The distributed nature of GIS has many implications for interoperability between multiple GIS organizations and systems. Collaboration among GIS users is crucial.

GIS users have long relied on collaborative efforts. Recent trends and efforts on GIS standards—such as the initiatives led by the Open Geospatial Consortium, Inc.® (OGC®) and the International Organization for Standardization (ISO) spatial standards committees—reflect this fundamental need.

Adherence to industry standards and commonly adopted GIS practices is critical to the success of any GIS. A GIS must support critical standards and adapt and evolve support as new standards emerge.

Many geographic datasets can be compiled and managed as a generic information resource and shared among a community of users. In addition, GIS users have envisioned how sharing these commonly used datasets can be accomplished through the Web.

GIS Web servers can be used to serve geographic information Web services in a services oriented architecture that integrates multiple heterogeneous systems supporting various types of GIS as well as numerous other IT-based Web services frameworks.

This vision has been in existence for more than a decade, and it has been described as a National Spatial Data Infrastructure (NSDI) or a Global Spatial Data Infrastructure (GSDI). These concepts are in general use today, not only at national and global levels, but also within states and local communities. This concept is collectively referred to as a Spatial Data Infrastructure (SDI).

A spatial data infrastructure is a federation of user sites that discover, use, and publish shared geographic information on the Web.

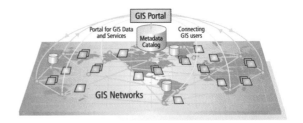

Geographic knowledge is inherently distributed and loosely integrated. GIS users can discover, access, and use inofrmation across the Web from many information nodes.

GIS collaboration

A GIS can be configured and deployed in many frameworks—for personal use, in workgroups, in departments, across an enterprise, and as a node in a federated GIS network that spans many organizations.

In this context, a GIS can be increasingly thought of as IT infrastructure for assembling large, sophisticated, multiuser systems. Yet, a GIS must simultaneously support the requirements of smaller workgroups and individual users.

A GIS platform must provide all the capabilities necessary to support this enlarged vision:

- A professional GIS desktop for authoring, editing, working with, analyzing, and visualizing geographic information.

- A geographic database to store and manage all geographic objects.

- A Web-based GIS server framework for distributed geographic information management, analysis, sharing, and use.

- A software developer's toolkit for assembling any GIS application and for integrating GIS with other

technologies across desktops, servers, custom applications, and mobile devices.

- A range of mobile application solutions for taking GIS into the field.

- An open, standards-based architecture and interoperability tools to work with many data types, interoperate using web services, and to work on an enterprise service bus architecture and within any services-oriented framework

- An interface to real-time sensor networks to support situational awareness as sensor information changes through time.

The ArcGIS product line was built to satisfy these evolving requirements and to deliver a scalable, comprehensive GIS platform.

ArcGIS is engineered for interoperability. It builds on both IT and GIS standards. All ArcGIS products are assembled from modular software components that enable common GIS logic to be used in professional GIS desktops, enterprise GIS servers, embedded in custom applications, and taken to the field in mobile devices.

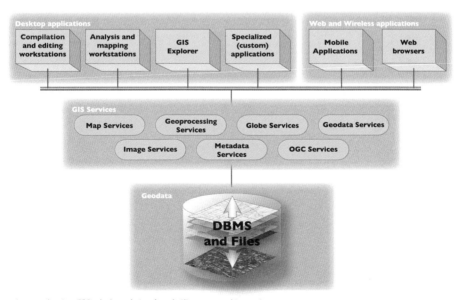

A comprehensive GIS platform designed to facilitate geographic requirements

2 What is ArcGIS?

GIS technology has long been valued for improving communication and collaboration in decision-making, for effectively managing resources and assets, for enhancing the efficiency of workflows, for improving the accessibility of information, and generally offering tangible cost savings to organizations both large and small.

In an effort to deliver geospatial information and functionality throughout an enterprise, organizations are choosing to extend their desktop GIS implementations with server-based GIS solutions and Web services. In addition, focused sets of GIS logic can be embedded and deployed in custom applications. And increasingly, GIS is deployed in mobile field devices.

THE CHANGING ROLE OF GIS

Traditionally, GIS professionals have concentrated primarily on data compilation and focused application projects, investing time in creating GIS databases and authoring geographic knowledge. Users apply comprehensive GIS workstations for compiling geographic datasets, building workflows for data compilation and quality control, authoring maps and analytical models, and documenting their work and methods.

This is the traditional view of a GIS user with a professional workstation connected to datasets and shared databases. The workstation has a comprehensive GIS application with advanced GIS logic and tools that are used to accomplish GIS tasks.

Progressively, more and more GIS professionals have begun to use and exploit their results in numerous GIS applications and settings.

The work of authoring and serving geographic knowledge will largely remain within the domain of GIS professionals. However, these professionals will also increasingly create server-based systems that allow others in their organizations (and in some cases, society at large) to have access to the power of GIS.

This means that the influence of GIS is growing and will provide a powerful medium for managing, visualizing, and communicating about our world.

The ArcGIS product line provides a scalable, comprehensive GIS platform to meet these requirements, as illustrated in the diagram below.

ArcGIS

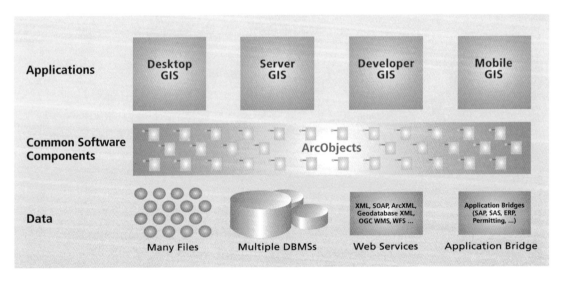

ArcGIS is a complete GIS software system for authoring, serving, and using geographic knowledge.

ArcGIS provides a scalable framework for implementing GIS for a single user or many users on desktops, in servers, over the Web, and in the field. ArcGIS is an integrated family of GIS software products for building a complete GIS. It consists of four primary frameworks for deploying GIS:

ArcGIS Desktop—An integrated suite of professional GIS applications comprised of three main software products: ArcView®, ArcEditor™, and ArcInfo®.

Server GIS—ArcIMS, ArcGIS Server, and ArcGIS Image Server

Mobile GIS—ArcPad and ArcGIS Mobile for field computing

ESRI Developer Network (EDN℠)—Embeddable software components for developers to extend GIS desktops, build custom GIS applications, add custom GIS services and Web applications, and create mobile solutions.

DESKTOP GIS

ArcGIS Desktop is the primary application used by GIS professionals to compile, author, and use geographic information and knowledge. It is available at three functional levels—ArcView, ArcEditor, and ArcInfo.

ArcGIS Desktop includes an integrated suite of comprehensive desktop applications—ArcMap, ArcCatalog™, ArcToolbox™, and ArcGlobe™. Each application has a rich set of GIS tools and operators.

ArcGIS Desktop can also be extended by purchasing a range of optional extensions that add specialized capabilities. For example:

• The Spatial Analyst extension adds raster geoprocessing and modeling.

• The 3D Analyst extension adds many 3D GIS capabilities and visualization applications.

• The Data Interoperability extension adds the ability to directly use dozens of GIS data formats in ArcGIS.

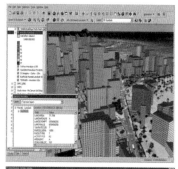

ArcGlobe

ArcMap

Two of the applications included in ArcGIS Desktop.

SERVER GIS

Much like the enterprise software evolutions witnessed in the financial, human resources, supply chain, and customer management arenas, GIS has evolved to meet enterprise-wide needs, supporting mission critical capabilities and robust architectures associated with other enterprise software and infrastructure.

Server GIS provides the basis for building an integrated, multi-departmental system for collecting, organizing, analyzing, visualizing, managing, and disseminating geographic information. Server GIS solutions are intended to address both the collective and individual needs of an organization and to make geographic information and services available to both GIS and non-GIS professionals.

The principal purposes of a Server GIS are to provide:

- Broad access to geographic information.

- A common infrastructure upon which to build and deploy GIS applications.

- A common GIS data management framework.

- Significant economies of scale and business value through organization-wide deployment and use of GIS.

The ArcGIS product family includes three server products—ArcIMS, ArcGIS Server, and ArcGIS Image Server. ArcIMS and ArcGIS Server share a common Web mapping application for building browser-based GIS applications.

ArcGIS includes three server products

ArcIMS—A scalable Web mapping server for GIS publishing of maps, data, and metadata using open Internet protocols. ArcIMS is deployed in tens of thousands of organizations and is used primarily for GIS Web publishing, delivering data and map services to many users on the Web, and hosting metadata catalog portals on the Web.

ArcGIS Server—A comprehensive Web-based GIS that provides a range of out-of-the-box end user applications and services for mapping, analysis, data collection, editing, and management of spatial information. ArcGIS Server provides a cost-effective, standards-based platform upon which ArcGIS Desktop users can easily publish and serve their geographic knowledge to the broader organization. ArcGIS Server supports access using a range of desktop, custom, mobile, and browser-based clients.

ArcGIS Server also includes the ArcSDE® data management technology for managing multiuser, transactional geodatabases using a number of relational DBMSs.

ArcGIS Image Server—An on-the-fly image processing server, ArcGIS Image Server provides very fast access to large image collections and significantly reduces the time between image acquisition and use. ArcGIS Image Server can create multiple products dynamically as a Web service and supports image access by a range of client applications.

DEVELOPER GIS

The ESRI Developer Network (EDN) is a developer product that provides a comprehensive system for developing applications with ArcGIS. EDN provides a unified programming environment and tools that enable developers to:

- Embed GIS and mapping functionality in other applications.

- Build and deploy custom ArcGIS Desktop applications and extensions.

- Configure and customize ArcGIS products, such as ArcView, ArcEditor, and ArcInfo.

- Extend the ArcGIS architecture and data model.

- Write custom applications using ArcGIS Engine.

- Build Web services and server-based applications using ArcGIS Server and ArcIMS.

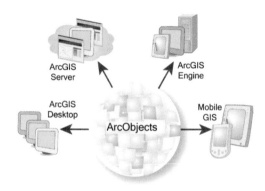

EDN includes all the developer resources of ArcGIS Desktop, ArcGIS Server, ArcIMS, ArcSDE, and the embeddable components of ArcGIS Engine.

The core of the EDN Developer Kit is a common library of software components, ArcObjects, that programmers can use to embed and extend GIS using standard programming environments such as C++, .NET, and Java®.

ArcGIS Engine

ArcGIS Engine is a developer product that provides a programming interface to use ArcObjects as a series of embeddable components with which developers can build focused applications with simple, custom interfaces. ArcGIS Engine provides a series of embeddable user interface components—for example, a Map Control and a Globe Control that can be used to embed interactive maps or globes in any application. Using ArcGIS Engine, developers can build focused GIS solutions using C++, .NET, or Java.

Developers can build complete custom applications with ArcGIS Engine or embed GIS logic into existing user applications—for example, to add a map to Microsoft® Word or Excel.

The use of custom applications is important for many GIS organizations to simplify and focus the use of GIS for numerous end users. For example, embedded GIS applications are used to support field data collection using Tablet PCs, custom interfaces for emergency operations, and structured data compilation workflows.

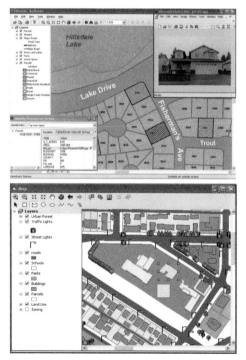

Use ArcGIS Engine to embed GIS into your applications.

MOBILE GIS

Increasingly, GIS is moving from the office into the field by means of focused application solutions on mobile devices. Wireless mobile devices enabled with global positioning systems (GPS) are increasingly used for focused data collection, map use, and GIS access in the field. Firefighters, waste collectors, engineering crews, surveyors, utility workers, soldiers, census workers, police, and field biologists represent a few types of field workers who use mobile GIS as a tool.

ArcGIS provides a comprehensive suite of mobile GIS products that are designed for different applications and platform requirements. These include:

ArcGIS Desktop and custom applications built using ArcGIS Engine. These are frequently deployed to the field on mobile laptops and Tablet PCs for users who need to work with geodatabases and detailed GIS maps.

ArcPad. ArcPad provides a rich environment for the GIS-centric field worker on Windows® CE-compatible devices. ArcPad is widely used in more than 60,000 deployments.

ArcGIS Mobile. ArcGIS Server 9.2 includes a software development kit, called ArcGIS Mobile, that can be used to create and deploy focused mobile applications for Smartphones, Pocket PCs, and Tablet PCs. These applications support wireless synchronization with ArcGIS Server, GIS data replication, and editing.

GIS can be taken into the field using a range of mobile devices and solutions.

THE GEODATABASE

The geodatabase is a collection of geographic datasets of various types used in ArcGIS and managed in either a file folder or a relational database. It is the native data source for ArcGIS and is used for editing and data automation in ArcGIS.

The geodatabase was designed as an open, simple geometry storage model and supports many possible storage mechanisms, such as

- Multiuser DBMSs—Oracle, Microsoft SQL Server, IBM DB2, and Informix®

- Personal geodatabases using Microsoft Access™

- File geodatabases that operate across a range of operating systems.

- Geodatabase XML for open exchange and interoperability

Geodatabases support much more than feature classes, images, and attributes. They are instrumental in implementing critical advanced GIS integrity rules and behavior using comprehensive data types such as topologies, networks, raster catalogs, terrains, cadastral fabrics, relationships, and domains.

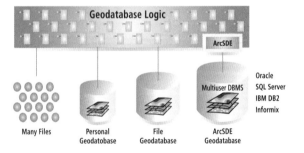

Geodatabases can be stored and managed in relational DBMSs, file systems, and Microsoft Access folders. Geodatabase application logic is also used to access and work with datasets in hundreds of formats and data structures.

3 Desktop GIS: ArcView, ArcEditor, and ArcInfo

ArcGIS Desktop is a comprehensive set of professional GIS applications used to solve problems, to meet a mission, to increase efficiency, to make better decisions, and to communicate, visualize, and understand an idea, a plan, a conflict, a problem, or the status of a situation.

In conducting this work, GIS users perform a number of tasks, including

- Working with maps

- Compiling, editing, and maintaining geographic data

- Automating work tasks with geoprocessing

- Analysis and modeling using geoprocessing

- Visualization and display of results in maps, 3D views, and dynamic, time-based displays

- Managing and maintaining multiuser geographic databases

- Serving GIS resources and results to a broad range of users for a multitude of applications

- Building custom applications to share GIS

- Documenting and cataloging their results—geographic datasets, maps, globes, geoprocessing scripts, GIS services, applications, and so on.

ArcGIS Desktop is the primary platform for GIS professionals to manage their complex GIS workflows and projects and to build data, maps, models, and applications. It's the starting point and the foundation to perform and deploy GIS across organizations.

ArcGIS Desktop includes a suite of applications including ArcCatalog, ArcMap, ArcGlobe, ArcToolbox, and ModelBuilder.

Using these applications and interfaces in unison, users can perform any GIS task, from simple to advanced.

ArcGIS Desktop is scalable and can address the needs of many types of users. It is available at three functional levels:

1. **ArcView** focuses on comprehensive data use, mapping, and analysis.

2. **ArcEditor** adds advanced geographic editing and data creation.

3. **ArcInfo** is a complete, professional GIS desktop containing comprehensive GIS functionality, including rich geoprocessing tools.

Additional capabilities can be added to all seats through a series of ArcGIS Desktop extension products from ESRI and other organizations. Users can also develop their own custom extensions to ArcGIS Desktop by working with ArcObjects, the ArcGIS software component library. Users develop extensions and custom tools using standard Windows programming interfaces such as Visual Basic® (VB), .NET, and Visual C++®.

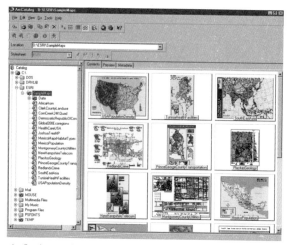

ArcCatalog provides an integrated and unified view of all the data files, geodatabases, maps, globes, and GIS services. It is also used to document and manage metadata.

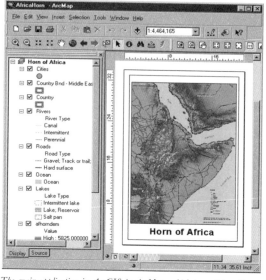

The main application in ArcGIS is ArcMap, which is used for all mapping and editing tasks as well as for map-based query and analysis.

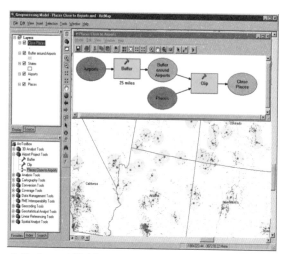

ArcToolbox and ModelBuilder are the cornerstones of the ArcGIS geoprocessing framework used for automating tasks and for spatial analysis.

ArcGlobe, an application included with the optional ArcGIS 3D Analyst extension, provides an interactive global view to work with geographic data in both 2D and 3D.

ArcMAP

The main application in ArcGIS is ArcMap, which is used for all mapping and editing tasks as well as for map-based query and analysis. It's the primary application for all map-based tasks including cartography, map analysis, and editing.

ArcMap is a comprehensive map authoring application for ArcGIS Desktop.

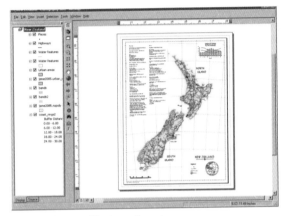

Design and create publication-quality maps.

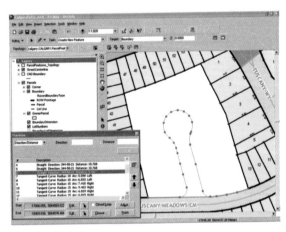

Compile and edit data.

ArcMap represents geographic information as a collection of layers and other elements in a map view. Common map elements include the data frame containing map layers for a given extent, plus a scale bar, north arrow, title, descriptive text, and a symbol legend.

There are two primary map display panels in ArcMap—the data frame and the layout view. The data frame provides a geographic "window" or map frame in which you can display and work with geographic information as a series of map layers. The layout view provides a page view where map elements (such as one or more data frames, a scale bar, and a map title) are arranged on a page.

ArcMap is the application used to compose maps on pages for printing and publishing.

Publishing ArcMap documents using ArcGIS Server

ArcMap documents (that is, interactive maps) can be published as GIS map services using ArcGIS Server. Maps are the primary ArcGIS service type. They are used for map serving and as the basis for mobile GIS deployments, editing, analysis, and workflow automation. Map services can be served using OGC WMS and KML.

Author and share maps with other applications such as ArcReader, ArcGIS Engine, ArcIMS, and ArcGIS Server.

Perform modeling and analysis.

ArcCATALOG

The ArcCatalog application helps users organize and manage all geographic information, such as maps, globes, data files, geodatabases, geoprocessing toolboxes, metadata, and GIS services. It includes tools to:

- Browse and find geographic information.

- Record, view, and manage metadata.

- Define, export, and import geodatabase data models.

- Search for and discover GIS data on local networks and the Web.

- Administer and manage ArcSDE geodatabases running in SQL Server Express.

- Administer and manage file and personal geodatabases.

- Administer and manage a series of GIS services.

Users can employ ArcCatalog to find, organize, and use GIS data as well as to document data holdings using standards-based metadata.

A GIS database administrator uses ArcCatalog to define and build geodatabases. A GIS server administrator uses ArcCatalog to administer the ArcGIS server framework.

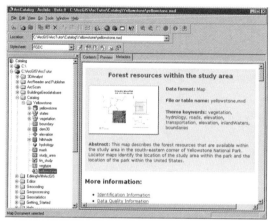

Metadata in ArcCatalog

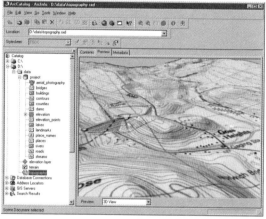

Previewing a 3D scene in ArcCatalog

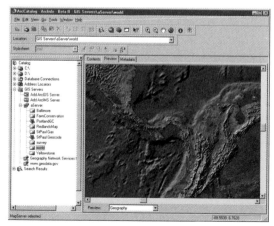

Previewing a map produced with ArcGIS Server in ArcCatalog

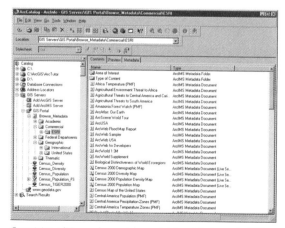

Organizing, editing, and managing a metadata catalog in an ArcIMS metadata server

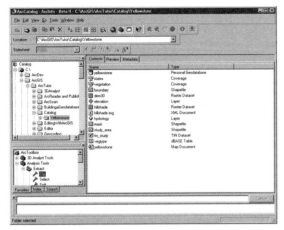

Geoprocessing in ArcCatalog

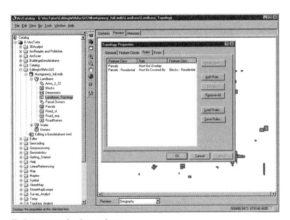

Defining a geodatabase schema

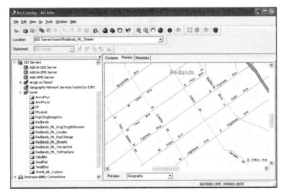

Managing map services in ArcGIS Server

GEOPROCESSING IN ArcGIS DESKTOP

Almost all uses of GIS involve the repetition of work, and this creates the need for methods to automate, document, and share multistep procedures known as workflows. Geoprocessing supports the automation of workflows by providing a rich set of tools and a mechanism to combine a series of tools in a sequence of operations using models and scripts.

Geoprocessing is based on a framework of data transformation. A typical geoprocessing tool performs an operation on an ArcGIS dataset (such as a feature class, raster, or table) and produces a new dataset as the result of the tool. Each geoprocessing tool performs a small yet essential operation on geographic data, such as projecting a dataset from one map projection to another, adding a field to a table, or creating a buffer zone around features. ArcGIS includes hundreds of such geoprocessing tools.

Geoprocessing allows you to chain together sequences of tools, feeding the output of one tool into another. You can use this ability to compose a variety of geoprocessing models (tool sequences) that help you automate your work, perform analysis, and solve complex problems.

ArcGIS Desktop provides a geoprocessing framework. This framework facilitates the creation, use, documentation, and sharing of geoprocessing models. The two main parts of the geoprocessing framework include:

- ArcToolbox, an organized collection of geoprocessing tools.

- ModelBuilder, a visual modeling language for building geoprocessing workflows and scripts.

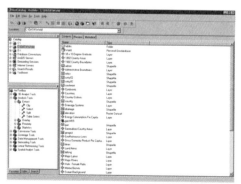

ArcToolbox is available in all ArcGIS Desktop applications such as ArcCatalog.

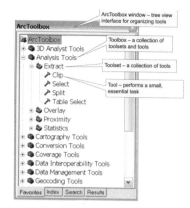

ArcToolbox is a comprehensive collection of geoprocessing functions organized into a collection of toolboxes.

Geoprocessing is included in ArcView, ArcEditor, and ArcInfo. Each product level includes additional geoprocessing tools:

- ArcView supports a core set of simple data loading and translation tools as well as fundamental analysis tools.

- ArcEditor adds a number of tools for geodatabase creation, loading, and schema management.

- ArcInfo provides a comprehensive set of tools for vector analysis, data conversion, data loading, and coverage geoprocessing.

Although geoprocessing is accessible in ArcView and ArcEditor, ArcInfo is the primary geoprocessing seat in a GIS organization because it contains comprehensive geoprocessing tools for performing significant GIS analysis. At least one ArcInfo seat is needed to build GIS data and perform analysis.

Additional geoprocessing toolsets come with many of the ArcGIS extensions, such as ArcGIS Spatial Analyst, which includes approximately 200 raster modeling tools, and ArcGIS 3D Analyst, which includes many triangulated irregular network (TIN) and terrain analysis tools.

Server-based geoprocessing

You can publish a toolbox as a geoprocessing service using ArcGIS Server to provide broad access to key automations, workflows, and analytical models.

This enables you to leverage geoprocessing on a server for managing data, publishing analytical models, and to automate key workflows.

MODELBUILDER

The ModelBuilder interface provides a graphical modeling framework for designing and implementing geoprocessing models that can include tools, scripts, and data. Users can drag tools and datasets onto a model and connect them to create an ordered sequence of steps to perform complex GIS tasks.

ModelBuilder provides an interactive mechanism for building and executing complex GIS procedures.

It is a productive way to share methods and procedures with others within, as well as outside, your organization.

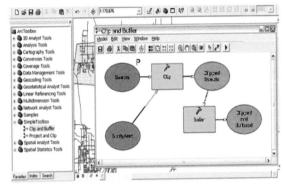

Models are data flow diagrams that string together a series of tools and data to create advanced procedures and workflows.

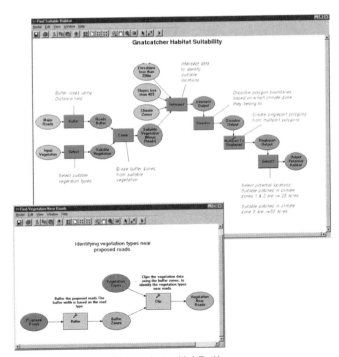

Examples of analytical models created using ModelBuilder.

ArcGLOBE

The ArcGlobe application is included in the optional ArcGIS 3D Analyst extension. It provides continuous, multiresolution, interactive viewing of geographic information. Like ArcMap, ArcGlobe works with GIS data layers, displaying information from geodatabases and all supported GIS data formats. ArcGlobe has a dynamic 3D view of geographic information. ArcGlobe layers are placed within a single global context, integrating all GIS data sources into a common global framework. It handles multiple data resolutions by making datasets visible at appropriate scales and levels of detail.

The ArcGlobe interactive view of geographic information significantly enhances a GIS user's ability to integrate and use disparate GIS datasets.

Publishing globe services in ArcGIS Server

Globe documents created in ArcGlobe can be published as GIS services using ArcGIS Server. These globe services are served over the Web, through ArcGIS Server, to a range of 3D clients—such as ArcGlobe and ESRI's new ArcGIS Explorer application that can be freely shared with anyone.

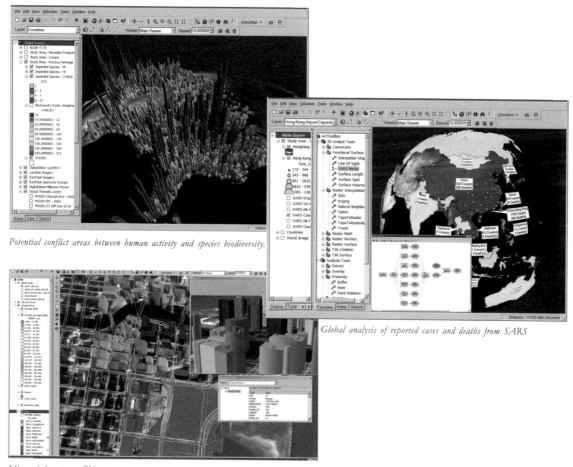

Potential conflict areas between human activity and species biodiversity.

Global analysis of reported cases and deaths from SARS

View of downtown Chicago

WHAT ARE ArcVIEW, ArcEDITOR, AND ArcINFO?

ArcGIS Desktop can be purchased as three separate software products, each providing increasing levels of functionality.

- ArcView provides comprehensive mapping, data use, analysis, and visualization tools along with simple editing and geoprocessing.

- ArcEditor includes advanced editing capabilities for shapefiles and geodatabases in addition to the full functionality of ArcView. ArcEditor also includes the ability to administer and use ArcSDE geodatabases in Microsoft SQL Server Express.

- ArcInfo is the full-function, flagship ArcGIS Desktop product. It extends the functionality of both ArcView and ArcEditor with advanced geoprocessing. It also includes the legacy applications for ArcInfo Workstation (ArcPlot™, ArcEdit™, ARC Macro Language [AML™], and so on).

Because ArcView, ArcEditor, and ArcInfo all share a common architecture, users working with any of these GIS desktops can share their work with other users. Maps, data, symbology, map layers, custom tools and interfaces, reports, metadata, and so on, can be accessed interchangeably in all three products. Users benefit from using a single architecture, minimizing the need to learn and deploy several different architectures.

In addition, maps, data, and metadata created with ArcGIS Desktop can be shared with many users through the use of ArcGIS Publisher and free ArcReader™ seats, custom ArcGIS Engine applications, and GIS Web services using ArcIMS and ArcGIS Server.

The capabilities of all three levels can be further extended using a series of optional add-on software extensions such as ArcGIS Spatial Analyst and ArcGIS Network Analyst.

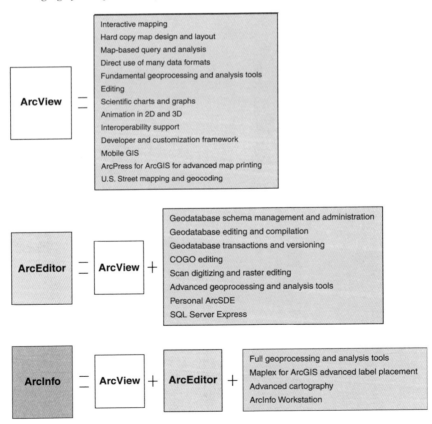

ArcView =
- Interactive mapping
- Hard copy map design and layout
- Map-based query and analysis
- Direct use of many data formats
- Fundamental geoprocessing and analysis tools
- Editing
- Scientific charts and graphs
- Animation in 2D and 3D
- Interoperability support
- Developer and customization framework
- Mobile GIS
- ArcPress for ArcGIS for advanced map printing
- U.S. Street mapping and geocoding

ArcEditor = ArcView +
- Geodatabase schema management and administration
- Geodatabase editing and compilation
- Geodatabase transactions and versioning
- COGO editing
- Scan digitizing and raster editing
- Advanced geoprocessing and analysis tools
- Personal ArcSDE
- SQL Server Express

ArcInfo = ArcView + ArcEditor +
- Full geoprocessing and analysis tools
- Maplex for ArcGIS advanced label placement
- Advanced cartography
- ArcInfo Workstation

WHAT IS ARCVIEW?

ArcView is the first of the three functional product levels of ArcGIS Desktop. ArcView is a suite of applications: ArcMap, ArcCatalog, ArcToolbox, and ModelBuilder. ArcView is a powerful GIS toolkit for data use, mapping, reporting, and map-based analysis.

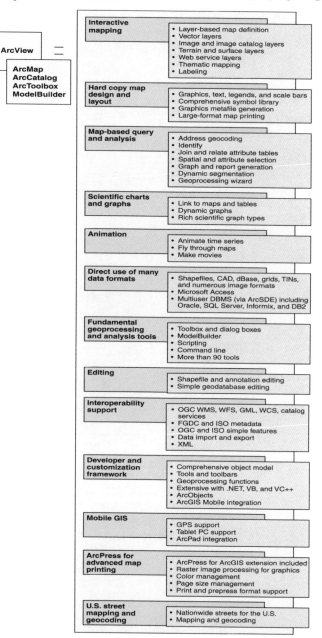

ArcView =
ArcMap
ArcCatalog
ArcToolbox
ModelBuilder

Interactive mapping
- Layer-based map definition
- Vector layers
- Image and image catalog layers
- Terrain and surface layers
- Web service layers
- Thematic mapping
- Labeling

Hard copy map design and layout
- Graphics, text, legends, and scale bars
- Comprehensive symbol library
- Graphics metafile generation
- Large-format map printing

Map-based query and analysis
- Address geocoding
- Identify
- Join and relate attribute tables
- Spatial and attribute selection
- Graph and report generation
- Dynamic segmentation
- Geoprocessing wizard

Scientific charts and graphs
- Link to maps and tables
- Dynamic graphs
- Rich scientific graph types

Animation
- Animate time series
- Fly through maps
- Make movies

Direct use of many data formats
- Shapefiles, CAD, dBase, grids, TINs, and numerous image formats
- Microsoft Access
- Multiuser DBMS (via ArcSDE) including Oracle, SQL Server, Informix, and DB2

Fundamental geoprocessing and analysis tools
- Toolbox and dialog boxes
- ModelBuilder
- Scripting
- Command line
- More than 90 tools

Editing
- Shapefile and annotation editing
- Simple geodatabase editing

Interoperability support
- OGC WMS, WFS, GML, WCS, catalog services
- FGDC and ISO metadata
- OGC and ISO simple features
- Data import and export
- XML

Developer and customization framework
- Comprehensive object model
- Tools and toolbars
- Geoprocessing functions
- Extensive with .NET, VB, and VC++
- ArcObjects
- ArcGIS Mobile integration

Mobile GIS
- GPS support
- Tablet PC support
- ArcPad integration

ArcPress for advanced map printing
- ArcPress for ArcGIS extension included
- Raster image processing for graphics
- Color management
- Page size management
- Print and prepress format support

U.S. street mapping and geocoding
- Nationwide streets for the U.S.
- Mapping and geocoding

A list of some of the key capabilities in ArcView. ArcView offers many exciting data use capabilities including advanced map symbology and editing tools, animation, scientific charting and visualization, metadata management, and on-the-fly projection.

WHAT IS ArcEDITOR?

ArcEditor is a GIS data automation and compilation workstation for the construction and maintenance of geodatabases, shapefiles, and other geographic information. ArcEditor, along with ArcInfo, enables GIS users to fully exploit the rich information model, advanced behaviors, and transaction support of the geodatabase.

ArcEditor provides all the capabilities of ArcView, as well as the ability to create and manage all types of geodatabases (personal, file, and ArcSDE geodatabases).

A copy of Microsoft SQL Server Express is included with ArcEditor. ArcCatalog is used to create and administer ArcSDE geodatabases in SQL Server Express. No DBMS administrator is required.

ArcEditor includes the ArcScan™ for ArcGIS extension for use in scan digitizing. ArcEditor also includes comprehensive geoprocessing tools for automating data management workflows and performing analysis.

Implementing a DBMS and accessing it via ArcSDE facilitates multiuser geodatabase editing and maintenance with complete version management in ArcEditor. This includes advanced tools for version management—for example, version merging tools to identify and resolve conflicts, perform disconnected editing, and conduct history management.

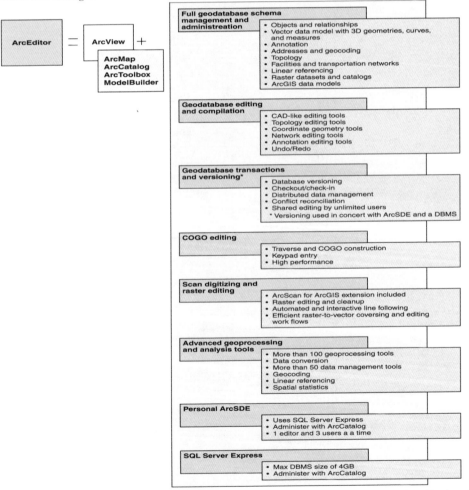

A list of some of the key capabilities of ArcEditor is shown above. ArcEditor offers the same functionality as ArcView but adds advanced editing.

WHAT IS ARCINFO?

ArcInfo is the flagship ArcGIS Desktop product. It is the most functionally rich client in ArcGIS Desktop. The high-end ArcInfo product provides all the capabilities of ArcView and ArcEditor. In addition, it includes a comprehensive collection of tools in ArcToolbox to support advanced geoprocessing and polygon processing.

The classic workstation applications and capabilities contained in ArcInfo Workstation, such as Arc, ArcPlot, and ArcEdit, are included as well. By adding advanced geoprocessing, ArcInfo is a complete system for GIS data creation, update, query, mapping, and analysis.

ArcInfo also includes the Maplex for ArcGIS extension.

Some of the most important types of operations performed in a GIS involve geoprocessing. Any organization requiring a comprehensive GIS needs at least one copy of ArcInfo to access its full geoprocessing capabilities to automate work and perform rich modeling and analysis.

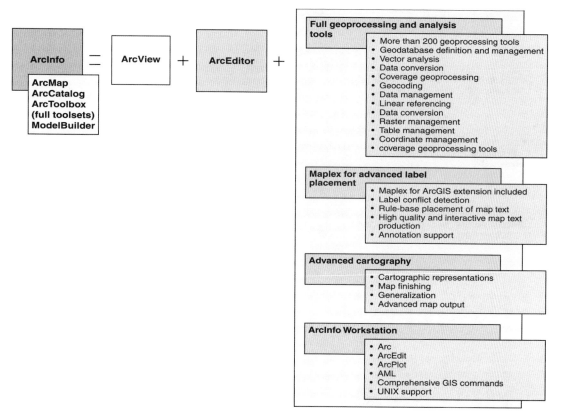

A list of some of the key ArcInfo capabilities is shown above. ArcInfo provides all the capabilities of ArcView and ArcEditor as well as additional geoprocessing functionality. The ArcInfo version of ArcToolbox is important for sites that build and create spatial databases and for advanced modeling and analysis.

OPTIONAL EXTENSIONS FOR ArcGIS DESKTOP

Many optional extensions are available for ArcGIS Desktop. Extensions allow users to perform tasks such as raster geoprocessing and three-dimensional analysis. All extensions can be used by each product—ArcView, ArcEditor, and ArcInfo.

The ArcScan for ArcGIS extension is included free of charge with ArcEditor and ArcInfo, and the Maplex for ArcGIS extension is also included with ArcInfo.

ArcGIS 3D Analyst
- ArcGlobe: Interactive 3D scenes
- Globe views in ArcCatalog
- Globe publishing in ArcGIS Publisher
- 3D raster and TIN modeling tools
- Publish globe services
- LIDAR and terrain datasets

ArcGIS Business Analyst
- Customer and store prospecting
- Market penetration analysis
- Drive-time analysis
- Business and demographic data

ArcGIS Data Interoperability
- Directly read, transform, and export any data format
- Tools for data transformation and direct use

ArcGIS Geostatistical Analyst
- Advanced kriging and surface modeling
- Exploratory spatial data analysis tools
- Probability, threshold, and error mapping

ArcGIS Network Analyst
- Network and transportation analysis
- Minimum path, closest facility, allocate, and traveling salesman
- Advanded network data modeling and simulation

ArcGIS Publisher
- Publish Map and Globe documents for use with free ArcReader application
- Package and compress data
- Optional data compression and locking
- Developer SDK for customizing ArcReader

ArcGIS Schematics
- Database-driven schematic rendering and display
- Schematic views of GIS networks and tabular information
- Multiple schematic representations

ArcGIS Spatial Analyst
- Advanced raster and vector tools
- Spatial modeling
- ArcGrid Map Algebra

ArcGIS Survey Analyst
- Comprehensive survey information management using the geodatabase
- Advanced survey computation
- Improved GIS data accuracy via links to survey locations
- Cadastral data model and editing workflow

ArcGIS Tracking Analyst
- Time-based map display and rendering
- Playback tools (play, pause, forward, rewind)
- Work with time-based data (featured whose geometry or attributes move and change)

ArcScan for ArcGIS
- Integrated raster-vector editing
- Vectorizing features from raster
- Raster snapping

ArcGIS Services
- Subscriptions to free and for fee GIS Web services
- Access to rich data and GIS tools
- GIS services hosting
- On-demand GIS services

Maplex for ArcGIS
- Advanced label placement and conflict detection for high-end cartographic production
- Simplifies the labor-intensive placement of map text

ArcGIS 3D ANALYST

ArcGIS 3D Analyst enables effective visualization and analysis of surface data. With ArcGIS 3D Analyst, users can view a surface from multiple viewpoints, query a surface, determine what is visible from a chosen location on a surface, and create a realistic perspective image by draping raster and vector data over a surface. The core of the ArcGIS 3D Analyst extension is the ArcGlobe application. ArcGlobe provides the interface for viewing multiple layers of GIS data and for creating and analyzing surfaces.

ArcGIS 3D Analyst also provides advanced GIS tools for three-dimensional modeling such as cut/fill, line of sight, and terrain modeling.

Support for terrain datasets

You can also create and manage terrain datasets using ArcGIS 3D Analyst. A terrain dataset is a multiresolution, TIN-based surface built from z measurements stored as features in the geodatabase. They're typically made from LIDAR, SONAR, and photogrammetric sources and can easily support billions of x, y, z points as part of a multiresolution triangulated surface.

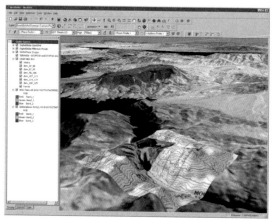

ArcGIS 3D Analyst includes three-dimensional visualization and terrain modeling capabilities.

ArcGIS 3D Analyst offers animation tools and functionality.

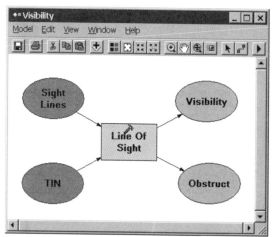

An example of TIN analysis using geoprocessing

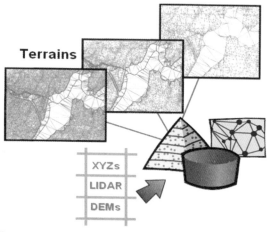

Terrains datasets can be created and managed in the geodatabase using ArcGIS 3D Analyst.

ArcGIS BUSINESS ANALYST

ArcGIS Business Analyst provides advanced analysis tools and a complete data package for analyzing business and demographic information as an aid in making critical business decisions.

ArcGIS Business Analyst includes an extensive collection of business, demographic, and consumer household data and tools for analyzing the market and competition, finding the ideal site for a new business location, or targeting direct mail. ArcGIS Business Analyst lets users perform sophisticated business analysis.

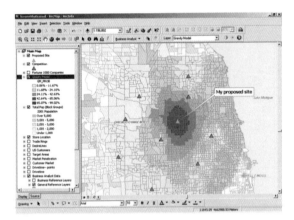

By combining information, such as sales data, demographics, and competitor locations, with geographic data, such as census boundaries, territories, or store locations, ArcGIS Business Analyst helps users better understand their market, customers, and competition.

ArcGIS Business Analyst allows users to:

• Choose site locations.

• Identify and reach potential customers.

• Find new markets.

• Perform customer or store prospecting.

• Define customer-based or store trade areas.

• Identify locations similar to that of their best stores.

• Conduct an analysis of market penetration.

• Create gravity models to forecast potential sales at new stores.

• Perform drive-time analysis over a nationwide street network.

• Search national businesses and add results to any analysis.

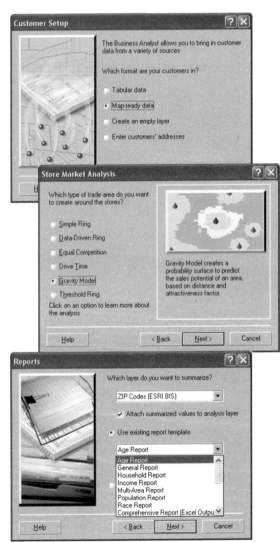

ArcGIS DATA INTEROPERABILITY

The ArcGIS Data Interoperability extension provides direct read access to dozens of spatial data formats, including GML profiles, DWG™/DXF™ files, MicroStation® Design files, MapInfo® MID/MIF files, and TAB file types. Users can drag and drop these and many other external data sources into ArcGIS for direct use in mapping, geoprocessing, metadata management, and 3D globe use. For example, you can make use of all the mapping functions available to native ESRI formats inside ArcMap for these data sources—such as viewing features and attributes, identifying features, and making selections.

The ArcGIS Data Interoperability extension was developed and is maintained collaboratively by ESRI and Safe Software Inc., the leading GIS interoperability vendor, and is based on Safe Software's popular Feature Manipulation Engine (FME®) product.

The ArcGIS Data Interoperability extension includes FME Workbench, which contains a series of data transformation tools to build converters for many complex vector data formats.

With the ArcGIS Data Interoperability extension, users can:

- Add support for many GIS data formats for direct use within ArcGIS, for example, for use in ArcMap, ArcCatalog, and geoprocessing.

- Connect to and read numerous common GIS formats—for example, TAB, MIF, E00, and GML—as well as numerous database connections.

- Manipulate and join rich attribute data from many table formats and DBMSs with features.

- Export any feature class to more than 50 output formats—for example, export to GML—and create advanced translators for custom output formats.

- Use the FME Workbench application to define additional formats and translation workflows.

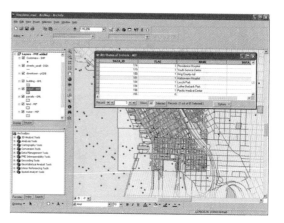

Users can drag and drop data sources into ArcMap and make use of all the mapping functions available to native ESRI formats, such as viewing features and attributes, graphing, and geoprocessing.

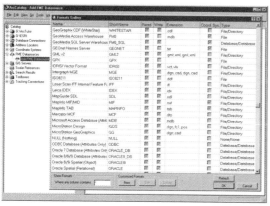

The formats gallery in the ArcGIS Data Interoperability extension provides access and direct use of dozens of GIS and tabular data formats.

ARCGIS GEOSTATISTICAL ANALYST

ArcGIS Geostatistical Analyst provides advanced statistical tools for surface generation and for analyzing and mapping continuous datasets. ArcGIS Geostatistical Analyst includes exploratory spatial data analysis tools that provide insights about your data distribution, global and local outliers, global trends, level of spatial autocorrelation, and variation among multiple datasets.

The ArcGIS Geostatistical Analyst extension's predictions can also measure uncertainty associated with predictions, allowing users to answer questions such as, What is the probability that the ozone levels exceed the Environmental Protection Agency (EPA) standard at the specified location?

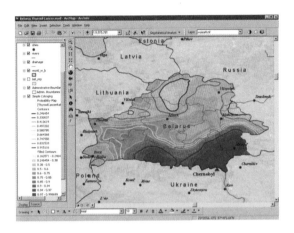

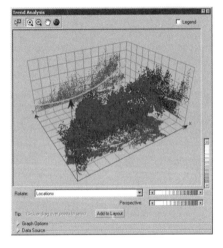

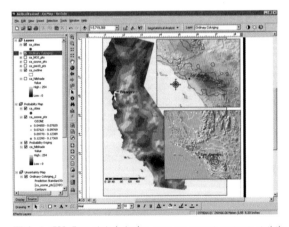

With ArcGIS Geostatistical Analyst, users can generate summary statistics, analyze trends, and graphically explore statistical data for surface estimation and generation.

ArcGIS NETWORK ANALYST

ArcGIS Network Analyst is an extension used for routing and network-based spatial analysis. ArcGIS Network Analyst allows ArcGIS Desktop users to model realistic network conditions and scenarios.

ArcGIS Network Analyst supports:

- Drive-time analysis

- Point-to-point routing

- Route directions

- Service area definition

- Shortest path

- Optimum route

- Closest facility

- Origin–Destination

ArcGIS Network Analyst enables ArcGIS users to solve a variety of problems using network datasets. Many network-based tasks can be performed, such as finding the most efficient travel route or closest facility, generating travel directions, and defining service areas based on travel time.

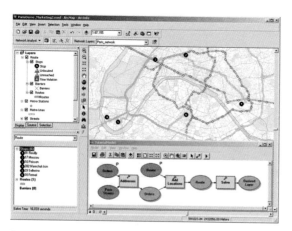
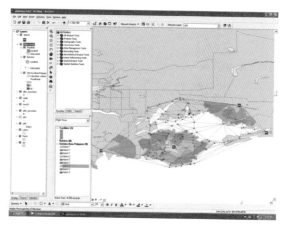

Route and travel time calculations performed with ArcGIS Network Analyst.

ArcGIS PUBLISHER and ArcREADER

ArcGIS Publisher is an extension used to publish data, maps, and globes authored using ArcGIS Desktop. ArcGIS Publisher enables the creation of a published map file (PMF) format for any ArcMap document as well as for any Globe document authored using the ArcGIS 3D Analyst extension.

PMFs are used in the free ArcReader application and allow users to share their ArcMap documents with other users. Using ArcGIS Publisher, datasets can be published, compressed, and locked in a high-performance, read-only file geodatabase format to allow secure access to sensitive or high-value geographic datasets.

Adding ArcGIS Publisher to ArcGIS Desktop allows users to open up access to their spatial information to many other users. With ArcMap and ArcGlobe, users can author interactive maps and globes, publish them with ArcGIS Publisher, and share them via ArcReader, ArcGIS Server, and ArcIMS ArcMap Server.

What is ArcReader?

ArcReader is a map and globe viewer that can be freely distributed to any number of users. The ArcReader application is included with the ArcGIS Desktop installation media for a number of platforms including Microsoft Windows, Sun™ Solaris™, and Linux® running on Intel® hardware.

ArcGIS Publisher includes a programmable ArcReader control for VB, Visual C++, and .NET developers. This enables users to embed ArcReader in existing applications or to build a custom ArcReader for viewing PMFs.

ArcReader helps users deploy their GIS in many ways. It opens up access to GIS data; presents information in high-quality, professional looking maps; and provides ArcReader users with the ability to interactively use and print maps, explore and analyze data, and view geographic information with interactive, 3D scenes.

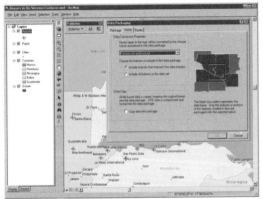

Build PMFs in ArcMap with the ArcGIS Publisher extension.

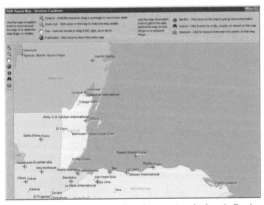

Deliver PMFs freely to any number of users using the free ArcReader application.

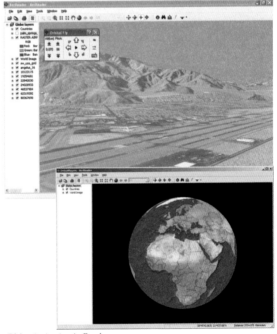

Globe viewing in ArcReader

ArcGIS SCHEMATICS

ArcGIS Schematics generates database-driven schematic and geoschematic graphic representations. Whether electrical, gas, telecommunications, or tabular networks, ArcGIS Schematics generates on-demand network graphs and schematics.

A schematic is a view of a GIS network. This extension enables users to draw many graphical views of a network structure and place schematic views in documents and maps.

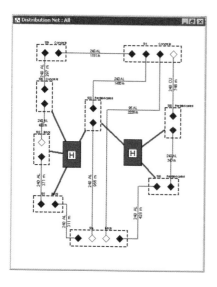

Some examples of ArcGIS Schematics for electric and water networks. In addition to infrastructure, social networks can be graphed and analyzed for applications such as disease surveillance and homeland security.

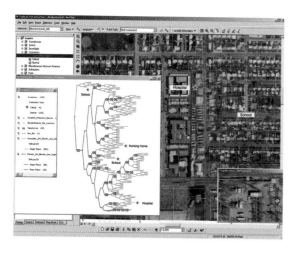

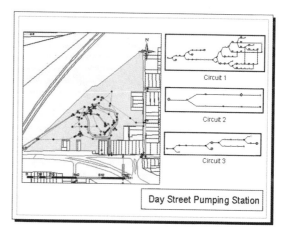

ArcGIS SPATIAL ANALYST

ArcGIS Spatial Analyst provides a broad range of powerful raster modeling and analysis features that allow users to create, query, map, and analyze cell-based raster data. ArcGIS Spatial Analyst also allows integrated raster–vector analysis. With ArcGIS Spatial Analyst, users can derive information about their data, identify spatial relationships, find suitable locations, and calculate the accumulated cost of traveling from one point to another.

ArcGIS Spatial Analyst provides a key toolbox of more than 200 raster geoprocessing functions that are used with the geoprocessing framework in ArcGIS Desktop.

The set of geoprocessing toolboxes included with ArcGIS Spatial Analyst.

Site suitability analysis

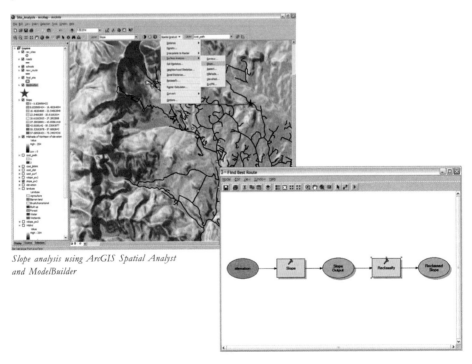

Slope analysis using ArcGIS Spatial Analyst and ModelBuilder

ArcGIS SURVEY ANALYST

The ArcGIS Survey Analyst extension includes tools used by surveyors and GIS professionals to create and maintain survey and cadastral data in ArcGIS.

With ArcGIS Survey Analyst, users can manage a comprehensive survey database as an integrated part of their GIS, including adding updates and improvements from new field surveys over time. The relative accuracy and error in the survey system can be displayed for any survey location. In addition, users can associate feature locations with survey points in the survey system and adjust feature geometry to snap to the survey locations.

ArcGIS Survey Analyst is used by GIS organizations to incrementally improve the spatial accuracy of their GIS data using survey techniques and GPS information.

Geographic feature geometry can be linked to survey locations to improve spatial accuracy.

Cadastral Editor

At ArcGIS 9.2, Survey Analyst includes support for a new workflow system for managing cadastral data as well as a new data model for managing cadastral fabrics. This data model includes specialized parcel topology and relationships between parcels, parcel boundaries, parcel corners, and control features. The new cadastral management workflow enables parcel measurement fabrics to be used to update existing map-based parcel frameworks. This includes applying a series of tools for coordinate and boundary entry, record and survey data entry, cadastral data management, and least squares adjustment. This system allows related GIS data to be adjusted using the same least squares adjustment parameters that are used for updating the cadastral fabric and tracks the history of adjustments. It also includes methods and workflow tools for cadastral jobs—for example, incrementally updating the cadastral or parcel fabric and related data as new surveys are added to the system.

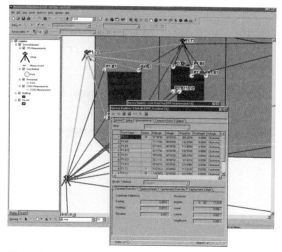

The graphic above shows measurement information and the traverse of the survey network.

ArcGIS TRACKING ANALYST

ArcGIS Tracking Analyst allows users to view and analyze temporal data; this includes tracking feature movement through time and tracking system values for locations over time.

ArcGIS Tracking Analyst includes:

- Display point and track data (real time and fixed time)

- The ability to symbolize time by color (to show the aging of data)

- Interactive playback

- Actions (based on attribute or spatial queries)

- Highlight capability

- Suppression

- Support for lines and polygons

- Temporal histogram in playback

- The ability to symbolize map layers based on time

- Layer-based time windows to manage many temporal layers

- Temporal offset for comparisons of temporal events

- Animation files

- Data clock for additional analysis

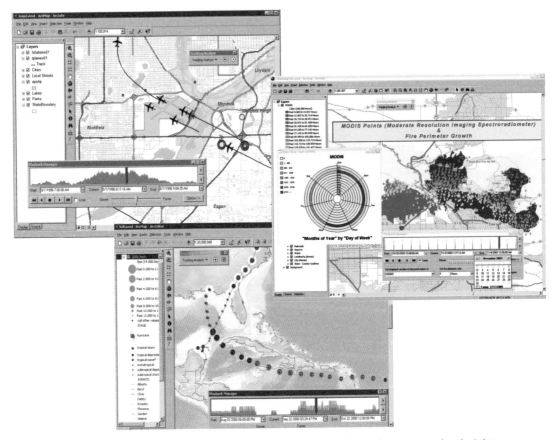

In ArcGIS Tracking Analyst, the interactive Playback Manager (start, stop, pause, rewind) is used to view events through windows.

ArcSCAN for ArcGIS

ArcScan for ArcGIS adds raster editing and scan digitizing functionality to the editing capabilities in ArcEditor and ArcInfo. It is used to generate data from scanned vector maps and manuscripts. It simplifies the data capture workflow of editing workstations using ArcGIS.

With ArcScan for ArcGIS, users can perform raster-to-vector conversion tasks, such as raster editing, raster snapping, manual raster tracing, and batch vectorization.

ArcScan for ArcGIS is included with ArcEditor and ArcInfo, and it is available as an optional extension for ArcView.

Floor plans

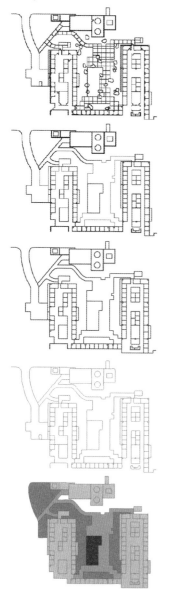

Soil maps

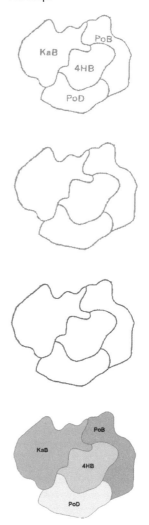

This workflow (top to bottom) shows vectorization examples of floor plans and soil maps. Results were achieved through a combination of raster editing and cleanup followed by scan digitizing.

MAPLEX for ArcGIS

Maplex for ArcGIS adds advanced label placement and conflict detection to ArcMap. Maplex for ArcGIS can be used to generate text that is saved with map documents as well as annotation that can be incorporated into comprehensive annotation layers in the geodatabase.

Using Maplex for ArcGIS can save significant production time. Case studies have shown that Maplex for ArcGIS can shave at least 50 percent, and often more, off the time spent on map labeling tasks. Because Maplex for ArcGIS provides better text rendering and print-quality text placement, it is an essential tool for GIS-based cartography. Any GIS site that makes maps should consider having at least one copy of Maplex for ArcGIS.

Maplex for ArcGIS is included with ArcInfo, and it is available as an optional extension for ArcView and ArcEditor.

Labels placed using the ESRI Standard Label Engine.

Labels placed with the Maplex for ArcGIS extension. With Maplex, you can place more labels, more accurately, in significantly less time.

4 Server GIS: ArcIMS, ArcGIS Server, and ArcGIS Image Server

Server GIS is growing rapidly because of its business advantages and its capability to leverage valuable GIS information and resources that are authored and managed by GIS professionals. In an effort to deliver geospatial information and functionality throughout an enterprise, organizations are extending their desktop GIS implementations with server-based GIS solutions that provide content and capabilities via Web services.

Users across an organization benefit from a shared implementation of GIS servers. GIS professionals with knowledge and expertise in specific domains can share their skills or disciplines with others—both GIS and non-GIS professionals. For example, a GIS transportation engineer who is an expert in multimodal transportation models can publish and share network solvers that can be consumed by other GIS professionals and users within the organization. Sharing geographic knowledge helps GIS users standardize geographic processing techniques and workflow scenarios, reduce software deployment costs, and ease implementation burdens.

GIS professionals not only use GIS servers as platforms to publish and promote their work in the form of shared maps, globes, geoprocessing models, and applications, they also consume services that are published by others in their GIS community.

GIS servers offer the following advantages:

- Significant economies of scale and business value through organization-wide deployment and use of GIS.

- Centrally managed and shared GIS computing resources that can be accessed by many.

- A range of client applications and tools that are flexible enough to support any task or mission—for example, browser-based access to GIS, mobile devices, editing applications, ArcGIS Explorer , and GIS desktop applications.

- Integration with other enterprise systems such as customer relationship management (CRM) or enterprise resource planning (ERP) systems using standards-based software interfaces and methods. GIS servers provide the foundation for geospatially enabling a services-oriented architecture (SOA).

- The ability to create custom applications using industry standard programming environments (for example, .NET, Java, AJAX, XML/SOAP, J2EE™, EJB, and C++).

- A common set of shared map and GIS services that ensures consistency in information management and a common operational view.

- GIS catalog services, data sharing, and data download services to orchestrate access to shared information.

- Support for interoperability standards in both the GIS domain (for example, OGC and ISO) and the broader information technology (IT) domains (for example, W3C and ISO).

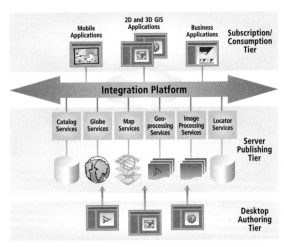

The adoption of Server GIS is growing rapidly because of its business advantages and its capability to leverage valuable GIS information and resources that are authored and managed by GIS professionals and used broadly across organizations.

ArcGIS offers three server products.

ArcIMS—A scalable Web mapping server for GIS publishing of dynamic maps, data, and metadata catalogs using open Internet protocols. The primary focus of ArcIMS is Web delivery of dynamic and scalable map services and metadata to many users. ArcIMS is designed for high-performance, open map publishing.

ArcGIS Server—A comprehensive Web-based GIS that provides a range of out-of-the-box end user applications and services for mapping, analysis, data collection, editing, and management of geospatial information. ArcGIS Server provides a cost-effective, standards-based platform upon which ArcGIS Desktop users can easily publish and serve their geographic knowledge to the broader community. ArcGIS Server supports access using a range of desktop, custom, mobile, and browser-based clients.

ArcGIS Image Server—An on-the-fly image processing server. Image Server provides very fast access to large image collections and significantly reduces the time between image acquisition and use. Image Server can create multiple products dynamically as a Web service and supports image access by a range of client applications.

ESRI's GIS servers comply with IT, Web, and GIS industry standards. They interoperate with other enterprise software, such as Web servers, DBMSs, enterprise application frameworks (such as J2EE and Microsoft .NET), and in services-oriented architectures.

This enables integration with other GIS technology as well as a range of information system technologies.

Capabilities		ArcIMS	ArcGIS Server	ArcGIS Image Server
Administration	Browser tools for server administration	X	X	X
	ArcCatalog tools for server administration		X	
Store, manage, and serve geographic information	Metadata Catalog services	X		
	2D map services	X	X	
	3D globe services		X	
	Geodatabase services		X	
	Image services			X
	Geoprocessing services		X	
	Geocoding services	X	X	
	Mobile map services		X	
	Network analysis services		X	
	Data interoperability services		X	
	Editing services		X	
Client applications	Browser-based Web mapping	X	X	
	Browser-based Web editor		X	
	ArcGIS Desktop	X	X	X
	ArcGIS Engine	X	X	X
	ArcGIS Explorer		X	
	ArcGIS mobile clients		X	
	Open clients	X	X	X
Interoperability support	OGC support	X	X	X
	ISO support	X	X	X
	W3C support	X	X	X
	Enterprise Service Bus and SOAP XML		X	

GIS functionality in the three ArcGIS server products

GIS WEB PUBLISHING OF MAPS, DATA, AND METADATA

ArcIMS stands for Arc Internet Map Server and provides dynamic Web mapping and metadata catalog services for many users both inside and outside an organization. ArcIMS is well known for providing highly scalable and high performance map services on the Web. It is the most widely used GIS server. It's estimated that the existing ArcIMS user community serves more than 100 million maps a day across more than 50,000 active ArcIMS services.

Typically, ArcIMS users access GIS Web services through their Web browsers—for example, by using the Web mapping application included with ArcIMS or using the traditional HTML and Java viewer applications included with ArcIMS in past releases.

In addition, ArcIMS services can be accessed using a wide range of clients including ArcGIS Desktop, ArcGIS Engine, ArcReader applications, ArcPad applications, ArcGIS Server Web mapping applications, and many open clients and devices that support XML and OGC WMS for Web communications.

ArcIMS also provides a metadata explorer application for searching metadata catalogs on the Web.

The Web mapping application included in both ArcIMS and ArcGIS Server.

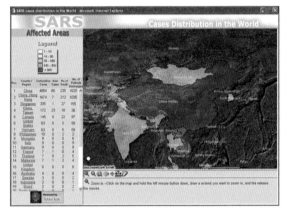

Java JSP application created using ArcIMS.

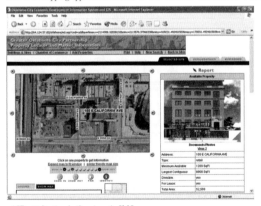

ASP application built using ArcIMS.

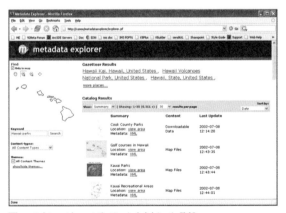

The metadata explorer application included in ArcIMS.

ArcIMS is used for GIS Web publishing to deliver maps, data, and metadata on the Web. Users most commonly access ArcIMS services using their Web browsers.

HOW IS ArcIMS USED?

ArcIMS applications share a set of common characteristics:

- There are many users.

- The application must be able to scale from minor to very heavy use (perhaps millions of Web hits per day).

- The interfaces to these applications are browser-based, simple, and focused.

- Users tend to do a small number of very focused, well-defined tasks, but expect high performance.

The primary focus of ArcIMS is Web delivery of GIS maps and metadata. The following three examples illustrate the main application functions of ArcIMS.

Focused application deployment

ArcIMS is most often used to deliver GIS to numerous internal users or external users on the Web. ArcIMS provides a simple, focused Web mapping application to access and use data using Web browsers.

Users perform basic tasks in these Web applications—for example, to view and interact with status maps of particular events and outbreaks (such as SARS and West Nile virus), or to provide a range of e-government services for citizens. E-gov applications might include parcel tax review, permitting, and mapping of high-interest public information such as crime, city development plans, school districts, voter polling places, and so on.

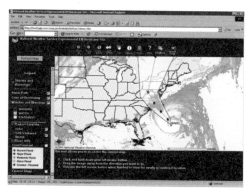

A National Weather Service Web site for hurricanes

A British Geological Survey Web site

Data access and publishing for professional GIS users

Many GIS groups publish a series of data feeds for GIS professionals within, as well as outside, their organization. Such ArcIMS applications are focused on data sharing between GIS professionals. The intended uses of the data vary from user to user. GIS professionals fuse this data into their GIS, along with other information sets, to accomplish many tasks.

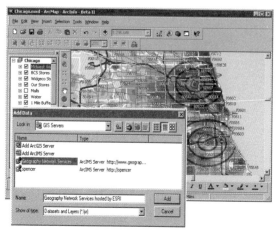

ArcGIS Desktop users access data using ArcIMS servers to enrich maps and integrate remote information into their daily work.

Technology for building **GIS catalog portals**

Many GIS users recognize that GIS data moves through networks. A GIS network is a loosely coupled federation of GIS server nodes where GIS data and Web services are published by numerous organizations.

An exciting trend and vision in GIS is the development of national, continental, and global spatial data infrastructures (often referred to as NSDIs or GSDIs) where many users register their GIS datasets, information, and activities at a common catalog portal. The GIS catalog portal can be searched, much like an Internet search engine, to discover and gain access to GIS information relevant for specific purposes.

ArcIMS includes tools for building GIS portals with metadata catalogs, search and discovery services for the Web, data and metadata harvesting services, gazetteer services, and Web mapping applications.

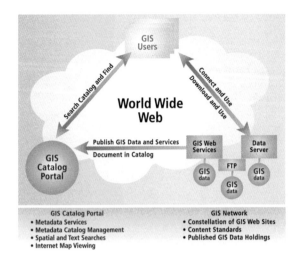

GIS networks enable users to connect to GIS catalog portals and to search for, find, connect to, and use geographic information on the Internet.

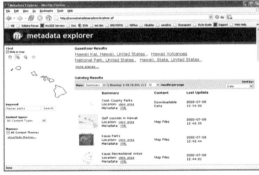

The Web-based metadata explorer is included with ArcIMS.

The **ESRI GIS Portal Toolkit**

The optional GIS Portal Toolkit is available for building and managing GIS catalog portals. Hundreds of organizations have published spatial data infrastructure nodes for their organizations using the GIS Portal Toolkit.

Metadata search applications and tasks that are included in ESRI's GIS Portal Toolkit.

ArcIMS CAPABILITIES

Some of the key GIS Web publishing capabilities of ArcIMS include the following:

Image rendering service

Delivers a snapshot of the map to the requesting client. Image rendering creates a snapshot of the current extent. For example, as a user pans and zooms on a map or turns map layers on and off, an ArcIMS map server renders each view and delivers it as an image to the ArcIMS client. This is the most widely used ArcIMS map service because of its high performance and scalability. The ArcIMS Image Service can use one of two protocols: ArcXML™ or the OGC WMS specification.

Feature streaming

Streams compressed vector features to the requesting client as a series of simple features (points, lines, polygons, and selected attributes). Feature streaming enables a number of client-side tasks: feature labeling, MapTip creation, spatial selection, and so on. Feature streaming is important for more advanced ArcIMS clients such as ArcGIS Desktop. Streamed features from ArcIMS Web sites can be integrated with other features, such as local data, and used together in analysis. Feature services can use one of two protocols: ArcXML or the OGC WFS specification.

ArcMap Image Service

Streams images from an ArcMap document to the requesting client. This service enables users to deliver maps that use the advanced cartographic and open data access capabilities of ArcMap. Virtually any information and graphic representations that are created in ArcMap can be served using ArcMap Server. ArcMap Server also supports access to versioned geodatabases and is used in many enterprise GIS scenarios. An ArcMap Image Service can use one of two protocols: ArcXML or the OGC WMS specification.

Data extraction

Select, extract, and package features as datasets for download and use. Users can request geographic datasets from the server. The server responds to a request for data by sending zipped data files in a selected format to the client (for example, as shapefiles) for local use.

Geocoding

Allows users to submit an address and receive a location from the ArcIMS geocoding service. The server either returns the location of an exact match to the address or a list of candidate matches.

Metadata catalog services

A catalog that references data holdings and information sets can be created using ArcGIS Desktop, ArcIMS, or ArcSDE and published as a search service using ArcIMS. This allows users to provide an open search mechanism for other users to find and access GIS information at their Web site. They can create a clearinghouse, and they can participate in a GIS network with other users.

Web mapping application

An out-of-the-box, ready-to-use Web map application that runs inside your Web browser. This supports multiple map services from ArcIMS, ArcGIS Server, OGC WMS, as well as ArcWeb Services published by ESRI. This application is also included with ArcGIS Server.

ArcIMS Web Manager

Used by non-developers to create and manage ArcIMS Web applications and to configure GIS tasks for use in ArcIMS. Using the ArcIMS Web Manager, you can select map services to display on your Web map, configure the GIS functions and tasks that users can access, and set the look-and-feel of your application's Web page.

Software developer kits (SDKs) for .NET and Java

Supports both .NET and Java developers. Includes controls and components of the Web mapping application.

Metadata explorer application

A browser-based application for searching and browsing GIS metadata catalogs. This also includes a customizable gazetteer. This application and toolset is important for building GIS catalog portals.

OGC interoperability support

ArcIMS supports many GIS and IT Web services standards. This includes broad ongoing support for many OGC specifications, such as WMS, WFS, WCS, and catalog services for the Web (CS-W).

OPTIONAL EXTENSIONS FOR ArcIMS

The Web publishing capabilities in a GIS Web site can be enhanced through a series of optional ArcIMS product extensions.

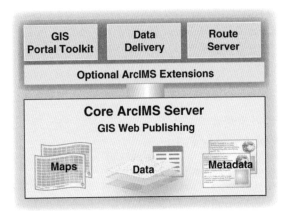

Optional extensions that add capabilities to ArcIMS Web sites

Data Delivery Extension

ArcIMS Data Delivery Extension enables ArcIMS sites to deliver data downloads in any number of GIS data formats, including complex data translators defined with the ArcGIS Data Interoperability extension. ArcIMS Data Delivery Extension is based on Safe Software's FME suite for advanced spatial data translation.

Route Server

The ArcIMS Route Server extension provides a countrywide navigation street database to support optimal routing and geocoding services on street data.

GIS Portal Toolkit

The GIS Portal Toolkit extension is a technology and services solution for implementing local, regional, national, and global SDI portals. GIS portals organize content and services such as directories, search tools, community information, support resources, data, and applications. They provide capabilities to query metadata records for relevant data and services and link directly to the online sites that host content services. The content can be viewed as maps and used in geographic queries and analyses.

ESRI's GIS Portal Toolkit provides all the tools and templates to create a GIS portal. Based on ESRI's ArcIMS and ArcSDE software, this standards-based solution offered through ESRI Professional Services is a cost-effective way to get a functional site up and running quickly.

The key elements of GIS Portal Toolkit are:

- Portal Web Site Template—A collection of template Web pages, scripts, and content that constitutes a functional draft of a GIS portal Web site. The template provides tools to perform a number of tasks, such as building a user interface to the site, hosting user-supplied content in the form of Web pages, and querying content.

- Map Viewer—A browser-based map data viewer that can combine data services from one or more portal servers. Map Viewer has extensive functionality for map navigation, printing, selection queries, data exploration, direct use of online Web services, and fusing multiple services into a single map.

- Metadata Catalog—A searchable repository that can store, update, and retrieve metadata.

DEVELOPING ArcIMS APPLICATIONS

ArcXML

ArcIMS uses XML for its communications and interactions. The openly published XML language for ArcIMS is called ArcXML. It provides access to all ArcIMS functions and capabilities. All client requests and server responses in ArcIMS are encoded in ArcXML.

Many ArcIMS developers program Web services and map specifications using ArcXML to customize and extend core ArcIMS capabilities. An application programing interface is provided for developers:

- The .NET ArcXML API for Microsoft developers

- The Java ArcXML API for Java developers

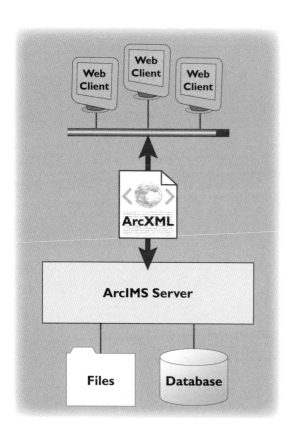

Web application SDKs

ArcIMS also includes a set of SDKs for customizing and extending the out-of-the-box Web mapping and metadata explorer applications that are included with ArcIMS. The SDKs include controls and components of the AJAX-based Web mapping application and the browser-based metadata explorer application. Developers can use individual Web controls and tools or use each application as a developer template. Each SDK supports both Microsoft .NET Visual Studio® and Java developer environments (such as Eclipse and Sun Java Studio Creator).

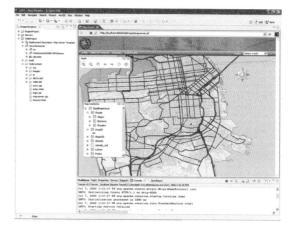

Using the Java Eclipse environment to customize the AJAX-based Web mapping application. AJAX (Asynchronous JavaScript and XML) combines a number of existing Web technologies to enhance the user experience in a Web browser. In essence, it enables a Web application to communicate with other resources (such as Web servers) while users continue to interact with the application. The Web mapping application SDK is also included as a developer tool with ArcGIS Server 9.2.

As in previous versions of ArcIMS, a series of connectors are also included that enable Web developers to use standard tools such as ColdFusion®, Active Server Pages (ASP) for Microsoft developers, and JavaServer Pages™ (JSP™).

The principal purposes of server GIS are to provide:

- Broad Web-based access to geospatial data.

- A common infrastructure upon which to build and deploy GIS applications.

- A common GIS data management framework.

- Significant economies of scale and business value through GIS deployment and use throughout an organization.

ArcGIS Server is a platform for building workgroup, departmental, and enterprise GIS applications that meet these goals. ArcGIS Server implementations are centrally managed, support multiple users, provide access to rich GIS functionality, and are built using industry standards.

ArcGIS Server provides a comprehensive Web-based GIS server that supports geographic data management, mapping, geoprocessing, spatial analysis, editing, and other GIS functionality across distributed systems.

A COMPLETE GIS SERVER

ArcGIS Server includes:

- Easy to configure Web applications

- Desktop client support for ArcGIS Desktop and ArcGIS Explorer

- A comprehensive set of GIS services

- Management and administration tools for configuring, publishing, and tuning your GIS server

- A comprehensive software developer toolkit for both .NET and Java developers

- A comprehensive application developer framework (ADF) for mobile clients.

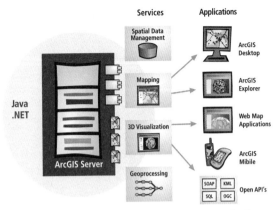

ArcGIS Server allows GIS professionals to publish GIS services and easily configure a range of GIS client applications.

Ready-to-use ArcGIS Web Services
2D and 3D mapping services
Geocoding services
Geoprocessing services for workflow automation and analysis
Geodata management services
Support for SOAP, OGC WMS, and KML

ArcGIS Server Developer Capablilities
AJAX-based Web applications
Mobile applications using Microsoft Windows Mobile developer technology
ArcSDE and SQL APIs for working with geodatabases
Out-of-the-box and custom Web services using SOAP
Integration with services-oriented architectures (SOAs)

THE ARCHITECTURE OF ArcGIS SERVER

The ArcGIS Server system incorporates the following components:

- **GIS server**—The GIS server hosts your GIS resources, such as maps, globes, geoprocessing tools, and address locators and exposes them as services to client applications.

  When a client application requests the use of a particular service, the GIS server generates a response and returns it to the client application. The GIS server can be configured to handle a number of simultaneous requests and can orchestrate how it responds efficiently to respond to those requests. This often involves configuring your GIS server to run on multiple machines.

- **Web server**—The Web server hosts Web applications and services that utilize the resources running on the GIS server.

- **Clients**—Client applications are Web, mobile, and desktop applications that connect over HyperText Transfer Protocol (HTTP) to Internet services or to local services over a LAN or WAN. Three specialized application frameworks are included with ArcGIS Server: 1) the Web mapping application, 2) the free ArcGIS Explorer application, and 3) ArcGIS Mobile.

- **Data server**—The data server contains the GIS resources that have been published as services on the GIS server. These resources can be map documents, address locators, globe documents, geodatabases, and geoprocessing toolboxes. Often, a relational DBMS is used to host an ArcSDE geodatabase in the data server tier to provide geodata scalability, security, integrity, and performance.

- **Manager and ArcCatalog administrators**—ArcGIS Server administrators can use either Manager or ArcCatalog to publish and administer their GIS resources and services.

  Manager is a Web application that supports GIS service and administration, Web application creation and management, and publishing of ArcGIS Explorer maps on the server.

ArcCatalog can be used to add connections to GIS servers for either general use or server administration. It also provides an interface for GIS professionals to publish their GIS resources as GIS services.

- **ArcGIS Desktop content authors**—To author the GIS resources such as maps, geoprocessing tools, and globes that will be published to your server, you will need to use ArcGIS Desktop applications such as ArcMap, ArcCatalog, and ArcGlobe.

The ArcGIS Server System Architecture

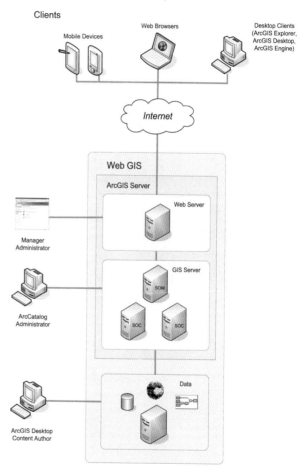

SERVING GIS RESOURCES OVER THE WEB

ArcGIS Server allows you to share your GIS resources across an enterprise and across the Web. GIS resources are the maps, globes, address locators, geoprocessing toolboxes, and geodatabases you want to share with others.

Author and publish using ArcGIS Desktop

ArcGIS Server 9.2 leverages ArcGIS Desktop by allowing GIS analysts to author maps, globes, and geoprocessing tasks on their desktops, then publish them to ArcGIS Server. Publishing can be performed inside ArcGIS Desktop using ArcCatalog. Alternatively, a browser-based application called ArcGIS Server Manager can be used to publish maps, globes, geoprocessing tools, and other GIS resources.

You can share these resources by first hosting them on ArcGIS Server as a Web service, then enabling a set of client applications (and other servers) to use and interact with the resources.

The main advantages of sharing your GIS resources on a GIS server are the same as sharing any data through the use of server technology—for example, the data is centrally managed, supports multiple users, and provides clients with up-to-date information and computing power they can access remotely.

Service capabilities

There are many types of ArcGIS services and each has certain capabilities that can be enabled. For example, if a map being published as a service contains a network dataset map layer, you can enable network analysis functions on that map service.

Optional Capabilities	What is enabled in the map service
WMS	Publishes a map service using the OGC Web Map Service (WMS) specification
KML	Publishes a map service using the Keyhole Markup Language (KML) specification
Mobile Data Access	Allows creation of mobile map data for use on a mobile device
Network Analysis	Solves transportation network analysis problems using the Network Analyst extension
Geodata Access	Provides geodatabase transaction support for replication and data extraction
Geocoding	Provides address geocoding support

Optional map service capabilities

TYPES OF SERVICES

Map services

A map service provides access to the contents of an ArcMap document (.mxd). To create a map service, you must first create the map document in ArcMap, then publish it as a map service.

Creating a map cache (optional)

A map cache is a collection of prerendered map tiles that can be used for high performance map display and use. Cached services display quickly because the map image does not have to be rendered on the fly at the time the user requests it. Instead, the rendering of the map image is precomputed when the map cache is created. Map caches are useful for serving map content that is static.

Cached Map Service   **Dynamic Map Service**

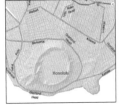 

1.5 Seconds   4 Seconds

Use of a map cache greatly improves performance and scalability.

Map caches involve map use for a range of map scales each containing appropriate levels of detail and resolution. Good map design for interactive maps will help to ensure that each map scale used will contain appropriate levels of detail. ArcMap and its scale dependent drawing capabilities are used to generate and maintain high performance map caches.

Extensible map service capabilities

The map service is the most common ArcGIS service to be published and contains a number of optional capabilities.

Many optional map service capabilities are enabled by including certain content in your map document. For example, if you want to edit geodatabase layers in a Web browser, you add them as map layers in ArcMap and publish the map as a Web service. Understanding how to create GIS resources with certain capabilities helps you leverage the power of ArcGIS Server.

Globe services

Globe documents that are created in the ArcGlobe application (which is part of the optional 3D Analyst desktop extension) can be published as globe services in ArcGIS Server. A globe service provides access to a 3D globe with which you can interact and integrate with other geographic information.

You can use globe services in ArcGlobe, ArcReader, and the new, free ArcGIS Explorer application. Globe services can also be published as KML services for use in other visualization applications.

Use ArcGIS Server to create your own virtual global views

Using ArcGlobe and ArcGIS Server, you can create complete virtual earth views in both 2D and 3D of any of your GIS data content and maintain it as information changes through time. Each GIS application often requires its own view of the information as well as access to specific tasks and operations. GIS users must be able to create systems that are tuned to work with specific content that can be visualized, analyzed, and understood.

The notion of publishing their own maps and globes is quite powerful and will have major implications as GIS professionals begin to serve their information to their end users as globes.

ArcGIS Explorer

ArcGIS Explorer is a new geospatial information viewer powered by ArcGIS Server. It offers a free, fast, and easy-to-use way to explore geographic information—in both 2D and 3D—with the ability to perform query and analysis tasks on the underlying data.

ArcGIS Explorer integrates server-based geoprocessing applications with GIS datasets by accessing the full GIS capabilities of ArcGIS Server, including geoprocessing and 3D services. ArcGIS Explorer can also use local data layers and services from ArcIMS, ArcWeb Services, OGC WMS, and KML, making it open and interoperable.

ArcGIS Explorer can be downloaded and used by anyone for both personal and professional use.

ArcGIS Explorer integrates the world of GIS and accesses the full GIS capabilities of ArcGIS Server. With ArcGIS Explorer, you can:

- Explore data for the entire world seamlessly in 2D and 3D.

- Fuse your local data with data and services from ArcGIS Server, ArcIMS, Open Geospatial Consortium WMS, and ESRI-hosted ArcWeb Services.

- Perform GIS analysis using tasks such as visibility, modeling, proximity search, and demographic analysis.

- Answer geographic questions about the maps you generate and share the results with others.

- Use maps and data from your own secure servers and fuse data from multiple servers.

View of downtown Los Angeles

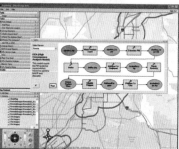

Modeling high consquence areas for emergency response

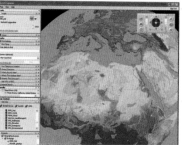

A global soils map

Example uses of globe services in the free ArcGIS Explorer application.

Geoprocessing services

The fundamental purpose of geoprocessing is to allow you to automate your GIS tasks. Almost all uses of GIS involve the repetition of work, and this creates the need for methods to automate, document, and share multistep procedures known as workflows. Geoprocessing also supports modeling and analysis, enabling you to better understand a problem, situation, or opportunity.

ArcGIS Server provides a simple mechanism that allows users to publish geoprocessing tools and models on servers and to make them available as tasks that can be executed on the server by many users from remote client applications.

GIS servers become very powerful when geoprocessing models and scripts are published as Web services. They are accessed and used by many who apply these tools, regardless of the client applications they use.

ArcGIS Explorer can access geoprocessing tasks that run remotely on ArcGIS servers.

In the example above, a trace is performed on an electrical network to troubleshoot a particular incident. This is initiated as a task in ArcGIS Explorer. A request is sent from ArcGIS Explorer to a geoprocessing service on ArcGIS Server that performs an analysis. The result is returned as a graphical display in the 3D map and as a report on the diagnosis and location of the problem.

Geocoding services

Geocoding is the process of converting street addresses into spatial locations, usually in the form of coordinate values (points).

Many users require the ability to use their own geocoding services. In most cases, they are unable to get satisfactory results with generic, commercially available geocoding applications because

- Addresses change over time as cities grow and expand.

- Addresses come in many forms and styles, ranging from the common address format of house number followed by the street name and succeeding information, such as city name and postal zone.

- Many countries and locales have their own geocoding styles and methods.

- Many users need to find locations of alias names (for example, "The Colosseum").

- Some locales have a number of alternative addresses for certain locations.

All of these situations call for specialized geocoding solutions, and many ArcGIS users invest time in building, maintaining, and providing user-specific geocoding services to meet their organization's needs.

Adding a geocoding service in ArcGIS Server starts by creating an address locator in ArcGIS Desktop. A locator is a geodatabase dataset that contains a set of addressable features, an address style, and rules for how addresses are matched to features in order to assign locations. Address locators in ArcGIS can be updated and maintained through time.

Geodata services

A geodata service allows you to access a geodatabase through the LAN, WAN, or Internet using ArcGIS Server. The service enables the ability to perform geodatabase editing and replication operations, make copies using data extraction, and execute queries on the geodatabase. A geodata service can be added for any type of geodatabase including ArcSDE geodatabases, personal geodatabases, and file geodatabases. However, ArcSDE geodatabases are preferred for most enterprise settings to support security, integrity, performance, and scalability.

Geodata services are particularly useful in situations where you manage distributed geodatabases in many locations. For example, a company may want to set up ArcSDE geodatabases to manage database replicas in its Los Angeles and New York offices. Once created, each office can publish its ArcSDE geodatabase on the Internet using a geodata service. The geodata services can then be used to periodically synchronize the updates across each geodatabase over the Internet by sharing only the changes between the two database servers.

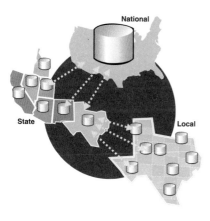

Geodata services are useful for synchronizing updates between a series of distributed ArcSDE geodatabase replicas.

WHY IS ArcSDE TECHNOLOGY INCLUDED IN ArcGIS SERVER?

An enterprise GIS is an integrated, multi-departmental system intended to address both the collective and individual needs of an organization and to make geographic information and services available to GIS and non-GIS professionals. Data servers contain the GIS resources that are published as services. For most GIS servers, this content is managed in relational databases using the geodatabase and ArcSDE.

To meet this need, ArcSDE technology and its ability to manage contents and transactions on multiuser geodatabases is a critical capability in every ArcGIS Server implementation. To support this, ESRI has integrated ArcSDE technology into ArcGIS Server.

Here are some of the advantages and capabilities provided by ArcSDE:

- High performance and systems scalability

- Integration with IT systems

- Reconcile on update with conflict detection

- Replication

- History archiving

- Versioned and non-versioned editing

- Cross-platform and cross-DBMS support of all functions

- SQL access to Oracle, IBM DB2, and Informix geodatabases

WEB MAPPING APPLICATION

ArcGIS Server includes an out-of-the-box, ready-to-use Web mapping application that runs inside your Web browser. This client provides a rich user experience for working with ArcGIS Server and other services.

This Web mapping application is also included as part of ArcIMS 9.2.

The Web mapping application supports the ability to fuse multiple map services from ArcIMS, ArcGIS Server, and OGC WMS, as well as ArcWeb Services published by ESRI.

Some of the application's tools and capabilities include:

- An interactive table of contents.

- Smooth map navigation, pan, and zoom.

- Map tips and feature identification.

- Tools for spatial query and selection.

- Web editing of ArcSDE geodatabases (such as adding features, split, snapping, reshape, and attribute updates).

- Easy to configure using ArcGIS Server Manager. No application programming is required.

- Rich developer environment for .NET and Java developers. Customizable as a series of programmable controls and components.

- Standards-based and open.

The Web mapping application architecture is based on AJAX, which combines a number of existing Web technologies that enhance the user experience. It enables a Web application to communicate with other resources (for example, Web servers) while users continue to interact with the application.

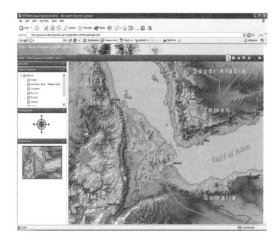

The Web mapping application included with ArcGIS Server.

ArcGIS MOBILE

ArcGIS Server 9.2 offers an application developer framework (ADF) known as ArcGIS Mobile that can be used to create and deploy focused mobile applications that operate in a "sometimes connected" environment and can be deployed to a large number of users.

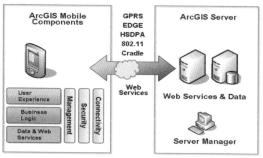

ArcGIS Mobile is a Microsoft Mobile developer's toolkit for ArcGIS Server.

These applications support mobile mapping, GPS, wireless synchronization, GIS data replication, and editing capabilities on a range of field devices running Microsoft Windows Mobile technology.

ArcGIS Mobile supports editing against versioned ArcSDE geodatabases in both connected and disconnected workflows. Periodically, you can synchronize updates directly with ArcGIS Server without returning to the office.

ArcGIS Mobile runs on a range of mobile devices: Smartphones, Pocket PCs, and Tablet PCs.

ArcGIS Mobile works on a range of field devices.

ArcGIS SERVER FOR DEVELOPERS

As you learn to use ArcGIS Server, you'll probably want to build customized applications or extend the out-of-the-box capabilities of ArcGIS Server. To meet this need, ArcGIS Server includes a comprehensive series of developer tools and capabilities.

In addition to providing out-of-the-box Web applications and services, ArcGIS Server can be used as a platform for developing Web and enterprise applications and services.

ArcGIS Server includes a full software development environment for:

• Microsoft .NET Framework

• Java platforms

Both platforms support a number of comprehensive developer tools for Web applications and services.

The Microsoft .NET development environment also includes a developer kit for the Web mapping application and mobile applications, while the Java development environment includes a developer kit for Enterprise JavaBeans™ (EJBs).

In addition, the Java tools support cross-platform development that can run on Windows, Sun Solaris, and Linux computers.

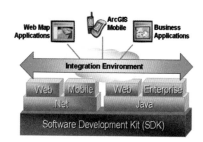

ArcGIS Server includes developer frameworks for both .NET and Java.

To meet the needs of workgroups, departments, and enterprises of all sizes, ArcGIS Server offers a scalable line of server products that are differentiated by both functionality and server capacity that can fit within any budget.

THREE FUNCTIONAL LEVELS OF ArcGIS SERVER

There are three levels of functionality for ArcGIS Server: Basic, Standard, and Advanced. To better assist the geographic data management needs and requirements of server users, ArcSDE technology is included with all three levels of ArcGIS Server.

- **Basic**—This edition provides users with a comprehensive GIS server for spatial data management. It focuses on organizing and managing geographic datasets using ArcSDE technology.

- **Standard**—This edition provides users with a comprehensive GIS server for spatial data management and visualization (mapping). This includes 2D mapping, 3D rendering (globe) services, and a suite of related features such as geocoding, gazetteer, and routing. Application developers have access to components (objects, Web controls, and services) for building solutions on both the Java and .NET frameworks. All aspects of the Basic edition are included in the Standard edition.

- **Advanced**—This edition provides users with a comprehensive GIS server for spatial data management, mapping, 3D visualization, and browser-based editing, as well as geoprocessing, spatial analysis, and modeling. All aspects of the Basic and Standard editions are included in the Advanced edition. For developers, the Advanced edition includes multitiered components for building and deploying both Java and .NET applications and services for desktop, mobile, smart client, Web browser, and enterprise deployments.

	Basic	Standard	Advanced
Multiuser Geodatabase	YES	YES	YES
Web-based Replication	YES	YES	YES
Web Mapping	NO	YES	YES
Globe Server	NO	YES	YES
Geoprocessing	NO	Limited	YES
Web-based Editing	NO	NO	YES
ArcGIS Mobile Application	NO	NO	YES

The three functional levels at which ArcGIS Server is offered—Basic, Standard, and Advanced. Each level adds further capabilities.

Two levels of server capacity

For each functional edition of ArcGIS Server, there are two use levels that define capacity. These levels are:

- **ArcGIS Server Workgroup**—This level is designed and limited to run on a single machine with a single CPU socket (single or dual core) and includes the Microsoft SQL Server Express database engine to support geodatabases.

- **ArcGIS Server Enterprise**—This level is designed to run on one or more machines and can scale beyond two sockets per machine. ArcGIS Server Enterprise includes ArcSDE; however, the user must acquire a DBMS (SQL Server, IBM DB2, Informix, or Oracle).

ArcGIS Server Workgroup		
Basic	**Standard**	**Advanced**
ArcSDE Data Management *SQL Server Express (10 user limit)*	**ArcSDE Data Management** *SQL Server Express (10 user limit)*	**ArcSDE Data Management** *SQL Server Express (10 user limit)*
Web GIS *Single server*	**Web GIS** *Single server*	**Web GIS** *Single server*
Geodata services for data replication services, versioning, check-in and check out	Geodata services for data replication services, versioning, check-in and check out	Geodata services for data replication services, versioning, check-in and check out
	• Map services • Globe services • Geocoding services • Limited geoprocessing • OGC Web services • Web-based mapping, applications, and templates • Developer tools (.Net & Java)	• Map services • Globe services • Geocoding services • OGC Web services • Web-based mapping, applications, and templates • Developer tools (.Net & Java)
		• Web-based editing • Geoprocessing services • Create tasks for Web clients • Mobile client developer toolkit
Single Computer Limited to a Single CPU Socket (With 1 or 2 Cores)		

ArcGIS Server Enterprise		
Basic	**Standard**	**Advanced**
ArcSDE Data Management *Oracle, SQL Server, IBM, DB2, Informix (No user limits)*	**ArcSDE Data Management** *Oracle, SQL Server, IBM, DB2, Informix (No user limits)*	**ArcSDE Data Management** *Oracle, SQL Server, IBM, DB2, Informix (No user limits)*
Web GIS *Single server*	**Web GIS** *Single server*	**Web GIS** *Single server*
Geodata services for data replication services, versioning, check-in and check out	Geodata services for data replication services, versioning, check-in and check out	Geodata services for data replication services, versioning, check-in and check out
	• Map services • Globe services • Geocoding services • Limited geoprocessing • OGC Web services • Web-based mapping, applications, and templates • Developer tools (.Net & Java)	• Map services • Globe services • Geocoding services • OGC Web services • Web-based mapping, applications, and templates • Developer tools (.Net & Java)
		• Web-based editing • Geoprocessing services • Create tasks for Web clients • Mobile client developer toolkit
One or More Computer No Memory Limits Licensed per CPU or Core		

USING ArcSDE TECHNOLOGY IN ArcGIS SERVER

Accessing and using ArcSDE technology is included in all ArcGIS Server product levels. ArcSDE is supported for:

- ArcGIS Server Workgroup

- ArcGIS Server Enterprise

Workgroup ArcSDE technology is included with ArcGIS Server Workgroup

ArcGIS Server Workgroup includes ArcSDE support for SQL Server Express. With this server level, you can use SQL Server Express for up to 10 simultaneous Desktop users and editors (for example, users of ArcView, ArcEditor, ArcInfo, a custom ArcGIS Engine application, AutoCAD, and MicroStation) plus any number of additional server connections that can be supported by your configuration.

SQL Server Express is included as part of ArcGIS Server Workgroup. It is limited to running on 1 CPU or core with a maximum of 1GB RAM. Database size is limited to a maximum of 4GB.

As the administrator, you can use ArcEditor or ArcInfo to create, administer, and manage workgroup ArcSDE geodatabases. You can set up and manage these workgroup ArcSDE geodatabases using SQL Server Express within ArcCatalog. No extra database administration expertise is required.

Enterprise ArcSDE technology is included with ArcGIS Server Enterprise

This is the traditional ArcSDE technology that runs on Oracle, SQL Server, IBM DB2, and IBM Informix and can scale to databases of any size and number of users, running on computers of any size and configuration.

With ArcGIS Server Enterprise, users provide their own DBMS license. The DBMS is typically administered and managed by a database administrator (DBA).

ArcSDE technology is included in this enterprise package to work with Oracle, IBM DB2, and Informix across a range of computer platforms and with SQL Server running on Windows servers.

A series of optional extensions is available for ArcGIS Server that adds capabilities to the core system.

SPATIAL

The ArcGIS Server Spatial extension provides a powerful set of functions that allows you to create, query, and analyze cell-based raster data.

You can use the Spatial extension to derive information about your data, identify spatial relationships, find suitable locations, calculate travel cost surfaces, and perform a wide range of raster geoprocessing operations using ArcGIS Server. Models and tools created using the ArcGIS Spatial Analyst extension can be published as Web services using this extension.

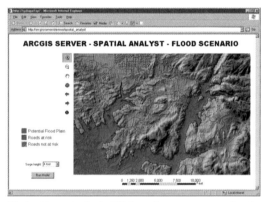

The Spatial extension for ArcGIS Server allows users to create and analyze cell-based raster data. Functions include viewshed, slope, aspect, hillshade analysis, and so on.

3D

The ArcGIS Server 3D extension provides a set of 3D GIS functions to create and analyze surfaces. The 3D extension adds a number of 3D and terrain-based geoprocessing operators that can be included in 3D modeling Web services.

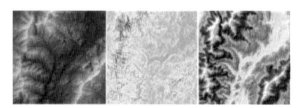

The 3D extension for ArcGIS Server provides a powerful set of tools that allows users to create, query, and analyze surface data.

NETWORK

The ArcGIS Server Network extension provides network-based spatial analysis capabilities including routing, travel directions, closest facility, and service area analysis. Developers can use it to build and deploy custom network applications.

The Network extension for ArcGIS Server provides tools for routing and network-based spatial analysis.

DATA INTEROPERABILITY

The ArcGIS Server Data Interoperability extension enables you to easily use and distribute data in many formats.

You can use the Data Interoperability extension to directly read more than 70 spatial data formats and export to dozens of spatial data formats. You can quickly translate between data formats using the Quick Import and Quick Export tools available in ArcToolbox. You can also perform sophisticated data transformations using the Workbench semantic translation engine and the Spatial ETL tool. ETL stands for Extract-Transform-Load and is used to transform data so it can easily move between a range of computing environments.

Special formats and translators built with the ArcGIS Data Interoperability extension can be used in ArcGIS Server Web services and geoprocessing services to support automated and open data interchange.

As the volume of imagery increases, GIS organizations are pressured to find solutions to provide this data to their users as quickly as possible. Often, the same source data is copied and processed several ways to produce different representations or image products (for instance, multiple band combinations, enhancements, or vegetative indexes).

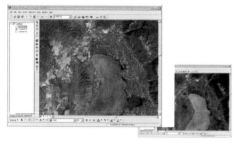

ArcGIS Image Server minimizes the time required to get imagery into production.

ArcGIS Image Server provides the ability to easily publish the latest imagery, without complex data loading or preprocessing. It gives GIS organizations the power to easily deploy multiple image products to many users while maintaining a single version of the source imagery.

Desktop Clients	Web Clients	Servers
• ArcGIS Desktop • AutoCAD • MicroStation • Open API • ERDAS IMAGINE • GeoMedia • MapInfo	• OGC WMS and WCS • KML via ArcGIS Server • SOAP via ArcGIS Server	• ArcIMS • ArcGIS Server

ArcGIS Image Server supports multiple clients and server frameworks.

Users can employ any of their existing imagery sources, including raster files on disks or rasters stored in a DBMS. The large collection of raster formats used by ArcGIS is directly supported.

In addition, ArcGIS Image Server provides extended support for the image metadata available from many commercial imagery sources (such as QuickBird, LANDSAT®, and many others), allowing important details, such as the date and time of acquisition, to be easily available.

ArcGIS Image Server dynamically processes the imagery. When administrators author a new service, they can define additional processes, such as pan-sharpening; band algebra; band combinations; stretching; sharpening; and terrain calculations (slope, aspect, and hillshade).

ArcGIS Image Server can perform these complex calculations in sub-seconds. This on-the-fly processing enables only one copy of the source data to be stored on the server; multiple representations of that imagery can then be served dynamically.

Four image server products produced from a single image source as image services.

KEY FEATURES OF ARCGIS IMAGE SERVER

- Fast access to extensive imagery

- Scalable enterprise client/server architecture

- Management of extensive volumes of imagery

- Direct access to multiple file formats and compression

- On-the-fly server-based image processing

- Creation of multiple imagery products from a single source

- Open GIS and Web client support

- Software developer kit

- Minimizes time and effort in making imagery accessible

- Increased value of imagery

Geometric Processing
Warping
Ground to image transform
• Affine
• Projective
• Warp Grid
• Orthorectification (separate extension)
Output to a specified projection
Imagery clipped to footprint or seamline
Definable sampling methods—Nearest neighbor, bilinear, cubic convolution
Single sampling from image to output
Mosaicking

Radiometric Processing
Extract/Stack bands from multispectral imagery.
Compute Normalized Digital Vegetation Index.
Histogram Stretching—Brightness, contrast, gamma.
Image Algebra—Image A (+,-,/,*) Image B,
Classify—Classify range values.
Colormap—Colorize index values.
Convolution Filter—Sharpen imagery.
Pan-Sharpen—Fuse panchromatic and multispectral bands.
Grayscale—Convert color to pan.
Spectral Matrix—Convert false color to pseudo color.
Elevation Visualization—Compute hillshade, slope, and aspect.
Trend—Apply trend to image.

Some of the on-the-fly image processing capabilities included in ArcGIS Image Server.

OPTIONAL IMAGE SERVER EXTENSIONS

ArcGIS Image Server has two optional extensions that provide focused image processing capabilities.

Orthorectification

This extension allows Image Server to dynamically orthorectify raw imagery using image properties and a terrain surface. The accuracy of this orthorectification can be updated at any time as photogrammetrists supply updated orientation parameters. This allows organizations to quickly publish imagery when speed and accessibility are critical and to refine the accuracy enhancements over time.

Seamline

This extension provides the ability to define and edit the irregular seamlines for overlapping image mosaics and specify a feathering that will be used along seamlines.

5

Developer GIS: ESRI Developer Network and ArcGIS Engine

Software development communities are becoming more important in helping to deploy GIS to a broad array of users. GIS developers support these deployments by building customized and focused applications that enable many end users to leverage the full capabilities of GIS.

One of the major goals of ArcGIS is to provide developers with a comprehensive series of developer frameworks to customize and deploy GIS. The name of this initiative is the ESRI Developer Network (EDN). EDN provides developer components, tools, and methods for the following GIS frameworks:

- Customizing and extending ArcGIS Desktop

- Building custom applications with embeddable GIS developer components using ArcGIS Engine

- Deploying custom Web applications and Web services using ArcIMS and ArcGIS Server

- Extending data types and accessing the contents of geodatabases, extending ArcSDE, and accessing relational DBMSs using SQL

- Building mobile applications and solutions for use with ArcGIS.

EDN includes all the developer resources of ArcGIS Desktop, ArcGIS Server, ArcIMS, ArcSDE, and ArcGIS Engine, as well as the embeddable components of ArcGIS Engine.

The core of the EDN Developer Kit is a common library of software components, ArcObjects, that programmers can use to embed and extend GIS using standard programming environments such as C++, .NET, and Java.

THE ArcOBJECTS SOFTWARE COMPONENT LIBRARY

The heart of ArcGIS development is the ArcObjects software component library. ArcObjects is an integrated collection of cross platform GIS software components that are client and server ready.

This shared library of ArcObjects provides a common developer experience across ArcGIS Desktop, ArcGIS Engine, and ArcGIS Server. It is built using a modular, scalable, cross platform architecture and offers a series of standard APIs for C++, .NET, and Java developers. ArcGIS provides a set of deployment options and resources for EDN developers.

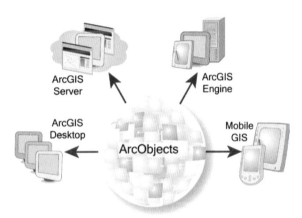

ArcObjects can be deployed in a number of frameworks. EDN provides the developer resources for all of these.

EDN represents a community of software developers who build and deploy applications with ArcGIS.

The goals of EDN are to:

*   Provide a complete system for GIS developers building on the ArcGIS platform.

*   Make ArcGIS developer technology easily available and affordable for developers through a single developer product.

*   Foster and support a vital GIS developer community.

EDN is available to all kinds of developers including commercial developers, consultants, systems integrators, and end use developers.

GIS developers can obtain the complete ArcGIS Developer Kit by subscribing to EDN. Each subscription covers the right to develop with ESRI software for 12 months and is renewable each year.

The annual EDN subscription includes the ArcGIS software library for the following products and developer resources, which can be used for creating a wide range of custom GIS applications and solutions:

*   ArcGIS Engine

*   ArcGIS Server (including ArcSDE and ArcGIS Mobile developer technologies)

*   ArcIMS

*   ArcWeb Services

The EDN subscription includes the ability to use any of these products for building, testing, and demonstrating custom applications. To deploy these applications, GIS end users need to buy appropriate software licenses for deploying the underlying ArcGIS software.

Technical support and instructor-led training for developers is optionally available as part of an EDN subscription. These options provide developers access to the developer support hot line, e-mail, and other technical support for dealing with developer issues.

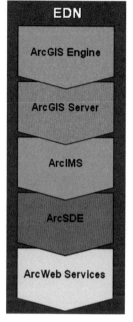

EDN is designed for developers who need low-cost access to ArcGIS technology for application development and customization. EDN is sold as an annual subscription and costs about the same as a copy of ArcView GIS.

There are three primary components necessary to begin development with the EDN software library. First, ArcGIS Desktop (ArcView, ArcEditor, or ArcInfo) is needed. ArcGIS Desktop is used to author geographic information elements such as datasets, maps, layers, geoprocessing models, and 3D globe projects that can be leveraged and embedded into custom applications using EDN. ArcGIS Desktop also provides the runtime environment for testing and demonstrating desktop applications and extensions. A special EDN product bundle includes an ArcView license for developers who do not already have access to ArcGIS Desktop.

Next, an annual subscription to the EDN program is required, which includes access to all the developer technology and resources for ArcGIS.

Finally, developers will need to determine what type of developer support they want. One option is to purchase direct phone support as part of EDN. Or the EDN Web site can be used to obtain developer help and support. Instructor-led training courses and technical consulting for EDN are also available.

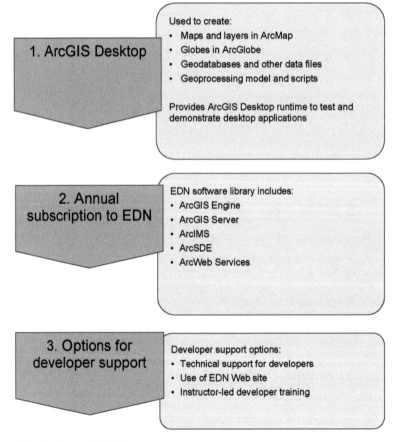

Effective development with EDN involves three components.

A companion Web site at *http://edn.esri.com* provides ongoing developer support and resources. The EDN Web site is a major component of the EDN program for supporting the ArcGIS developer community. It provides access to in-depth developer information such as code samples, technical articles, Webcasts, and e-mail alerts for subscribers. EDN developers can help one another by participating in developer forums and by sharing and reusing code from other developers in the EDN community.

Additional capabilities of the EDN Web site include the ability to download software updates, preview releases for developers, and receive invitations to special events for developers.

ESRI DEVELOPER SUMMIT

Each year, ESRI hosts a special conference for ArcGIS software developers called the Developer Summit. This conference includes numerous technical seminars for developers, opportunities to meet with ESRI development staff, and the chance to hear from developer experts from the ESRI Business Partner community and leading software developers from organizations such as Microsoft and IBM. Contact your ESRI sales representative for more information on this annual event.

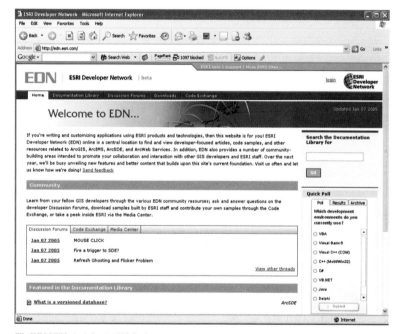

The EDN Web site is for ArcGIS developers.

EDN includes the ability to develop with all ArcGIS capabilities. Once an ArcGIS Desktop seat and an EDN subscription have been acquired, developers have access to the following capabilities:

ArcGIS DESKTOP

ArcGIS Desktop (ArcView, ArcEditor, and ArcInfo) can be customized with easy-to-use, drag-and-drop menu-driven tools or by using its extensible object model. Customizations can range from a simple command to a complex application extension. These represent the same methods that ESRI development teams use to build ArcGIS Desktop and its extensions.

Microsoft Visual Basic for Applications (VBA) and the ArcGIS Desktop developer kits are included with ArcGIS Desktop for scripting and application customization.

Developer kits for ArcGIS Desktop include support for:

* VBA

* Visual Basic 6

* .NET

* Visual C++

ArcGIS SERVER

Developers use ArcGIS Server to deliver advanced GIS functionality on the Web to a wide range of users. ArcGIS Server is built from the same modular, scalable, and cross platform ArcObjects components that comprise the ArcGIS system. ArcGIS Server provides developers with the ability to build advanced GIS services and Web applications in a server environment using an extensive set of developer kits.

Development capabilities for ArcGIS Server include:

* .NET and J2EE enterprise development frameworks.

* Out-of-the-box and extensible GIS Web services using XML/ SOAP and services-oriented architectures (SOAs).

* An AJAX-based Web browser application called the Web mapping application. This application can be used out-of-the-box or customized and extended using .NET or Java. The developer kit includes a Web application template and Web controls.

* ArcGIS Mobile, which is a developer kit for building mobile applications using the Microsoft Windows Mobile developer technology for mobile phones, Pocket PCs, and Tablet PCs.

* ArcSDE and SQL developer technology for accessing, working with, and extending geodatabases.

* The ability to host and serve geoprocessing tools as server-based tasks that can be accessed and used by any client (such as ArcGIS Explorer).

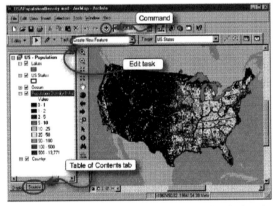

ArcMap interface illustrating some examples of how custom code and tools can be plugged into ArcGIS Desktop

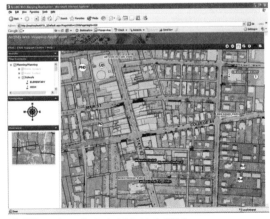

The Web mapping application included with ArcGIS Server.

ArcSDE technology included in ArcGIS Server

ArcSDE provides a number of options for building applications that work with and query information contained in multiuser geodatabases. In addition to the use of the ArcObjects component developer kit provided with ArcGIS Server (which provides developer access to the geodatabase object libraries), the ArcSDE Developer Kit is also included as part of the ArcGIS Server Developer Kit.

The ArcSDE Developer Kit includes a robust C API and a comparable Java API. In addition, the ISO and OGC SQL functions for spatial types are supported for use with Oracle, IBM DB2, and Informix DBMSs.

ArcIMS

ArcIMS developers work with ArcXML, the openly published communication protocol and Web API for ArcIMS, as well as a series of Internet connector technologies for building Web applications accessed through Web browsers. ArcIMS connector technologies for developers include ActiveX, .NET, Java, and ColdFusion.

ArcXML is the message protocol for communicating with ArcIMS. ArcXML is implemented as a series of requests and responses for interacting with an ArcIMS server, which provides the functional ArcIMS capabilities for serving maps and data in the appropriate format and sending these to the client.

ArcIMS also includes the same AJAX-based Web mapping application that is included with ArcGIS Server. This includes the developer components and developer kit for .NET and Java that can be used to customize and extend this browser-based application.

ArcIMS includes a new browser-based Web mapping application and developer kit. This AJAX-based application provides a rich user experience for working with GIS Web services. It is the same application that is included with ArcGIS Server and supports ArcIMS, ArcGIS Server, and OGC WMS services.

ArcGIS Engine is a core set of cross platform ArcObjects components compatible with multiple APIs such as .NET, Java, Visual Basic 6, and C++. Developers can use these embeddable components to build custom GIS and mapping applications. ArcGIS Engine applications can be built and deployed on Microsoft Windows, Sun Solaris, and Linux platforms. The applications can vary from simple map viewers to custom GIS editing programs.

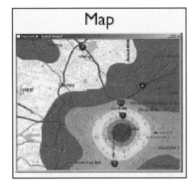

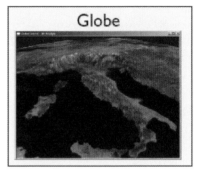

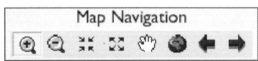

ArcGIS Engine includes a number of user interface controls and tools (in addition to the ArcObjects software libraries) for custom application development.

WHY USE ArcGIS ENGINE?

In many cases, users require GIS access through custom applications or through existing applications that contain focused GIS logic embedded into the application.

Users often require applications that run on UNIX® and Linux desktops in addition to Windows workstations. ArcGIS Engine is used to build these applications.

Typical customization examples using ArcGIS Engine include:

- Embedding GIS functions in word processing documents and spreadsheet applications—for example, adding a map control to Excel.

- Focused GIS field editing applications for Tablet PCs supporting a specific subset of advanced editing functions (a customized "ArcEditor Lite" application).

The ArcGIS Engine Developer Kit is a set of mapping components and developer resources that allows programmers to add dynamic mapping and GIS capabilities to existing applications or to build new custom mapping and GIS solutions. With ArcGIS Engine, developers have flexibility for creating customized interfaces for GIS deployment and use.

Developers can use one of several industry-standard, interactive development environments such as Microsoft .NET, C++, or Java to create unique applications or to combine the ArcGIS Engine components with existing software to create focused GIS applications.

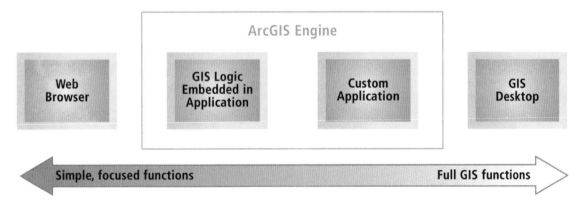

GIS clients can range from simple browser access to professional GIS desktops, such as ArcView and ArcInfo. ArcGIS Engine provides the capability to embed GIS logic in intermediate applications for end users who need access to rich GIS functionality.

Many applications require simple, focused user interfaces. However, they access advanced GIS logic to perform a few specific tasks. For example, many organizations have simple data editors that do not require a full GIS desktop.

Custom GIS applications are also typically tailored to a particular audience. The user interfaces are built to deliver GIS functions to many users not familiar with GIS.

To accomplish this, software developers require a programmable GIS toolkit that enables them to leverage common GIS functions in building their applications.

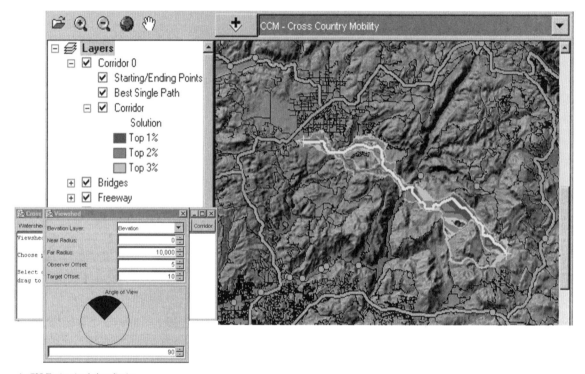

ArcGIS Engine viewshed application

WHAT IS INCLUDED IN ArcGIS ENGINE?

ArcGIS Engine is a comprehensive library of embeddable GIS components for developers to build custom applications. Using ArcGIS Engine, developers can incorporate ArcGIS functions into applications such as Microsoft Word and Excel as well as into custom applications that deliver focused GIS solutions to many users.

ArcGIS Engine runs on Windows, UNIX, and Linux desktops and supports a range of application development environments, such as Visual Basic 6, Visual C++, .NET, cross-platform C++, and Java developer environments including ECLIPSE™ and JBuilder®.

There are two parts to ArcGIS Engine:

- ArcGIS Engine Developer Kit is used by developers to build custom applications. This kit is part of the EDN software subscription.

- ArcGIS Engine Runtime is for end users to enable their computers to run applications containing ArcGIS Engine components.

ArcGIS Engine Runtime deployments are sold as separate runtime licenses for each software seat. ArcGIS Desktop is enabled to run ArcGIS Engine Runtime applications so users of ArcView, ArcEditor, and ArcInfo can run applications built with ArcGIS Engine. Other users who want to run ArcGIS Engine Runtime applications must purchase and install the ArcGIS Engine Runtime software.

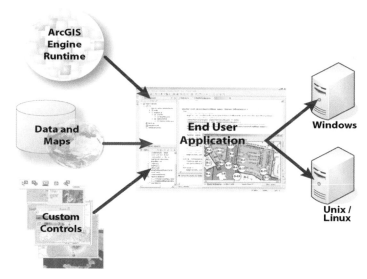

ArcGIS Engine is used by developers to build custom applications that can be deployed to many end users.

ArcGIS ENGINE DEVELOPER KIT

The EDN software library contains the ArcGIS Engine Developer Kit. This kit provides access to a large collection of ArcObjects components (the software components from which ArcGIS is built), including several developer controls for creating a high-quality mapping user interface and numerous tools for working with geographic information.

The visual controls are available as .NET controls, JavaBeans components, and as ActiveX controls. The Developer Kit is available for Windows, Linux, and Solaris operating systems and is a key part of the EDN product.

Programmers install the ArcGIS Engine Developer Kit on their computer and use it with their chosen programming language and development environment. ArcGIS Engine adds controls, tools, toolbars, and object libraries to the development environment for embedding GIS functions in applications.

Developing applications with ArcGIS Engine starts with authoring maps, data, and geoprocessing models with ArcGIS Desktop (ArcView, ArcEditor, or ArcInfo).

For example, an ArcView user creates and shares a map with an ArcGIS developer. The programmer can then build a custom application that contains the ArcMap document, some map tools from ArcGIS Engine, and other custom software functions.

Open support for programming languages and frameworks

ArcGIS Engine also provides support for C++, .NET, and Java, enabling developers to work with ArcGIS Engine in their chosen developer framework across a range of computer operating systems.

Windows	UNIX and Linux
C++	C++
Java	Java
Visual basic 6	
.NET	

ArcGIS Engine supports a number of computer platforms and programming languages.

Components of ArcGIS Engine Developer Kit

ArcGIS Engine Developer Kit includes three key collections of GIS logic:

- Controls

- Toolbars and tools

- Object libraries

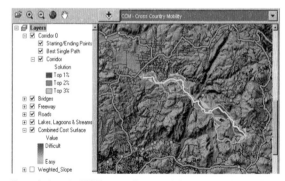

Example of an ArcGIS Engine application, including controls, toolbars, and objects.

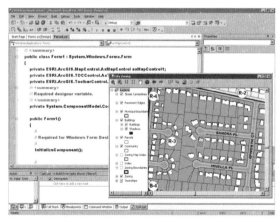

An example of a custom ArcGIS Engine application being developed with VB. A map control, a table of contents control, a menu, and a toolbar have been added to this VB form. The map control is associated with an ArcMap document (a .mxd file) used to draw and query interactive maps.

Controls

Controls are user interface components for ArcGIS that can be embedded and used in applications. For example, a map control and a table of contents control can be added to a custom application to present and use interactive maps.

Toolbars and tools

Toolbars contain collections of GIS tools for interacting with maps and geographic information in an application. Examples of tools used for interacting with maps include Pan, Zoom, Identify, Selection, and Editing. Tools are presented in the application interface using toolbars.

The process of building custom applications is simplified by having access to a rich set of commonly used tools and toolbars. Developers can simply drag-and-drop selected tools into custom applications or create their own custom tools for interacting with the map.

Object libraries

Object libraries are logical collections of programmable ArcObjects components, ranging from a geometry library to mapping, GIS data sources, and geodatabase libraries. Programmers use these libraries in their integrated development environments on Windows, UNIX, and Linux platforms to develop custom application code from simple to advanced. These same GIS libraries form the basis of ArcGIS Desktop and ArcGIS Server.

These ArcObjects libraries support all the comprehensive ArcGIS functions for developers and can be accessed through most commonly used development environments —for example, Visual Basic 6, C++, Java, .NET, and C#.

Example of the Map Navigation toolbar holding interactive tools for

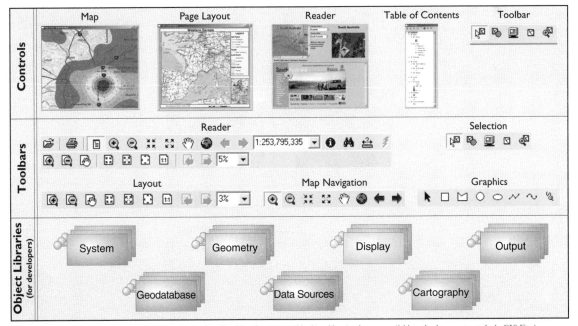

Illustration of some of the user interface components (controls and tools) and programmable object libraries that are available to developers as part of ArcGIS Engine.

ArcGIS Engine Runtime Extensions

ArcGIS Engine Runtime has a number of optional extensions that enable additional application programming capabilities. The functions supported by these extensions are similar to the ArcGIS Desktop extensions. In addition, each extension must be enabled for an ArcGIS Engine Runtime seat when they are used in a custom application.

Spatial

The Spatial extension adds comprehensive raster geoprocessing functions to the ArcGIS Engine Runtime environment. These additional capabilities are accessed via the ArcGIS Engine geoprocessing interface.

3D

The 3D extension adds 3D analysis and display functions to the ArcGIS Engine Runtime environment. Additional capabilities include Scene and Globe developer controls and tools, as well as a set of 3D object libraries for Scene and Globe.

Geodatabase Update

The Geodatabase Update extension adds the ability to edit and update any geodatabase using ArcGIS Engine applications. This is used to build custom GIS editing applications. These additional capabilities are accessed via an enterprise geodatabase object library.

Network

The Network extension provides a complete set of embeddable network analysis and modeling functions to ArcGIS Engine Runtime.

Data Interoperability

The Data Interoperability extension adds the ability to directly read and employ dozens of common GIS data formats, including many of the evolving GML specifications. It also enables delivery of GIS data to others in a variety of vector data formats.

Schematics

The Schematics extension enables generation, visualization, and manipulation of schematic diagrams from network data coming from a geodatabase or any data that has explicit attributes showing connectivity.

Maplex

The Maplex extension adds advanced label placement and conflict detection to map-based applications. This is used to generate text saved with map documents and as annotation layers in the geodatabase.

Tracking

The Tracking extension allows real-time and historic data display and temporal analysis.

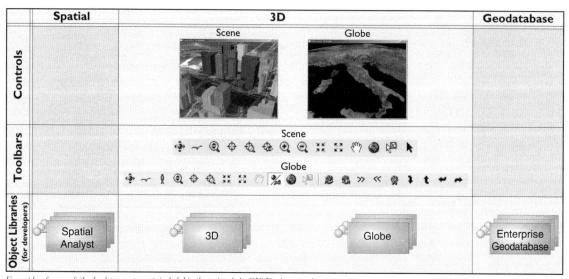

Examples of some of the developer components included in the optional ArcGIS Engine extensions.

DEVELOPING APPLICATIONS WITH ArcGIS ENGINE

Developers build ArcGIS Engine applications in their chosen integrated development environment (IDE), such as:

• Microsoft Visual Studio for Windows developers

• ECLIPSE, Sun ONE™ Studio, or Borland® JBuilder for Java developers

Developers register the ArcGIS Engine Developer components with their IDE, then create a forms-based application, adding in ArcGIS Engine components and writing code to build their application.

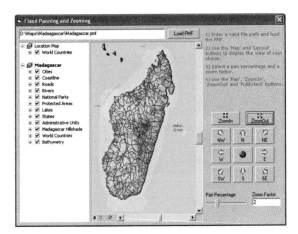

For example, a Java developer can build a focused GIS mapping application by adding a map control, a table of contents control, and selected toolbars to his or her application. The developer can associate an ArcMap .mxd file with the map control and program additional buttons and other functions for focused tasks. The finished application can then be deployed to many users.

DEPLOYING ArcGIS ENGINE APPLICATIONS

Once built, ArcGIS Engine applications can be installed on two types of ArcGIS seats:

• ArcGIS Engine Runtime seats that are enabled to run ArcGIS Engine applications

• Existing ArcGIS Desktop seats (that is, seats running ArcView, ArcEditor, or ArcInfo) that are equipped to run ArcGIS Engine applications

ArcGIS Engine Runtime can be installed and configured on many computers. An authorization file is required to enable ArcGIS Engine capabilities on each computer. The Runtime extensions to ArcGIS Engine can also be enabled by adding a line to the authorization file.

HOW IS ArcGIS ENGINE USED?

ArcGIS Engine is used to build a wide range of GIS applications and for embedding GIS into any application. Some GIS departments want to build focused GIS viewers with tools relevant for their end users. In other scenarios, just a piece of GIS is combined with other information tools for performing key tasks and workflows.

For example, a city government department may want to build a series of focused parcel review applications that access information from the GIS database, integrating it with critical enterprise work orders for permitting, taxation, planning review, and so forth.

ArcGIS Engine development environment

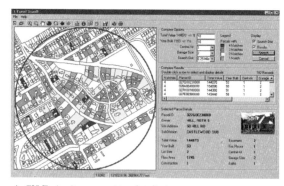

ArcGIS Engine city government parcel application

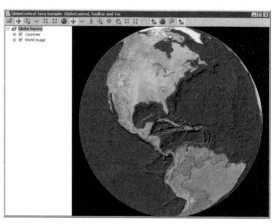

Some GIS organizations want to build custom applications for interactive globe viewing with the ArcGIS Engine 3D extension.

ArcGIS Engine components can be embedded in Microsoft Word documents and Microsoft Excel spreadsheets.

6 Mobile GIS using ArcPad and ArcGIS

Mobile computing is creating fundamental changes by adding the ability to take GIS with you into the field and interact directly with the world around you. Mobile GIS comprises the integration of a number of technologies:

- GIS

- Mobile hardware in the form of lightweight devices and ruggedized field PCs

- GPS

- Wireless communications for Internet GIS access

- Sychronization using GIS servers

Mobile GIS involves taking GIS to the field using a range of devices—Smart Phones, Pocket PCs, and Tablet PC devices.

MOBILE GIS APPLICATIONS

There are many types of mobile GIS applications. Here are some common examples:

Mapping and navigation systems—Provide low-accuracy and low-cost solutions for map-enabling a mobile application such as map use in the field. This often includes the ability to capture map notes.

Data collection systems—Provide accurate and professional solutions for field data collection that ensures the accuracy of your GIS data layers.

Survey systems—Provide highly-accurate and higher-cost solutions for field survey data collection. Surveying has not traditionally been considered a common part of GIS workflows; however, this is rapidly changing.

Traditionally, spatial information has been taken to the field using paper maps, often in the form of map books. Information collected with a map book in the field was sketched as notes on paper maps and entered into the GIS when the field worker returned to the office. Field

inspections were often performed using forms that were taken to the field, filled out on a clipboard, and entered into a database upon returning to the office. Data entry of paper information was inefficient, repetitive, and prone to error.

Organizations have begun to replace their paper-based systems with mobile applications. GIS-centric mobile applications, such as ArcPad, provide GIS software functionality that can be applied to a variety of field mapping and editing workflows. ArcPad is widely used in the GIS community for this type of fieldwork.

An increasing number of focused applications are also being developed and deployed. In many situations, a custom application is needed that focuses on specific tasks and workflows and simplifies the efforts to learn and use field-based GIS systems. ArcGIS Server and ArcGIS Engine provide effective tools for building easy-to-use, high performance mobile GIS applications.

ArcGIS offers a range of mobile solutions to meet these and a host of other requirements.

MOBILE GIS EXAMPLES

- Street sign inventory
- Power pole maintenance
- Meter reading
- Road pavement management
- Military fieldwork
- Mineral exploration
- Habitat studies and wildlife tracking
- Toxic inventory
- Crop management
- Property damage assessment
- Field surveying
- Incident reporting and inspection
- Real-time wildfire boundary mapping
- GIS data validation
- Building and asset inspection

MOBILE WORK TASKS

Here are some common tasks performed using mobile GIS.

Field map use—This type of application provides a way to take your geospatial information to the field as mobile maps to help you accomplish tasks in the field. A simple viewing application that enables query of asset information using a map adds value to field decisions. By adding navigational support using GPS, you can use map locations to zero in on information for field tasks. In these applications, users often add the ability to report locations to the office (for example, capturing and reporting the location of your mobile work force). This enables the ability to create an operational picture for your field workforce.

Field inspection—This type of mobile application helps field crews inspect assets in the field (for example, transformers, water meters, street signs, buildings, timber stands, and so on). Mobile workers report on each asset's condition and operational status, often taking a picture of the asset and using GPS to improve locational accuracy of features in the GIS.

Field data collection—This type of application is used to collect new information in the field with a streamlined data collection workflow. Often, the information that you collect and update in the field is only used to update one or two layers in your mobile map. For example, you may need to collect the locations of storm drains for a section of a city. However, within the map you will need to view the storm drains in association with other map layers that depict the storm sewer network, street centerlines, easements, block boundaries, and aerial photos. This information helps provide background information to support your data collection tasks. Building a mobile mapping application that displays background information and contains specific editing workflows helps to increase field worker productivity and reduces the training requirements for using the application.

Mobile developer tools can help organizations design, build, and deploy custom field applications that focus on helping each user get their job done.

GPS SUPPORT

A global positioning system (GPS) is a satellite-based navigation system made up of a network of 24 satellites placed into orbit by the U.S. Department of Defense. GPS was originally intended for military applications, but in the 1980s, the government made the system available for civilian use.

GPS uses radio signals broadcast from orbital satellites to calculate positions accurate to better than a centimeter given the right hardware. GPS has become a vital global utility, indispensable for modern navigation on land, sea, and air around the world.

Differential GPS (or DGPS) systems provide corrections to autonomous GPS positions supplying accuracies ranging from 5 meters down to sub-centimeter. DGPS systems rely on at least one GPS receiver located at a fixed point to calculate locational corrections to coordinates.

DGPS corrections are disseminated either in real-time or by post processing. Real-time DGPS is ideal for applications in the field that require high accuracy to navigate to features or to reposition them on the fly. However, for applications that require the highest possible accuracy, post processed DGPS is typically used.

ArcGIS Mobile products provide support for DGPS integration and use in order to achieve any level of accuracy that is needed in your mobile GIS applications.

Some field-based tasks involve fairly simple operations that require simple GIS tools. By contrast, some field-based tasks involve complex operations and detailed map views. Consequently, these advanced mobile applications require highly sophisticated GIS tools. A range of techniques and frameworks is needed to address these needs.

ArcGIS provides three product solutions for mobile applications that address both simple and sophisticated mobile requirements. These include:

- **ArcPad.** A mobile GIS application for taking GIS to the field. ArcPad is GIS-centric and focuses on field tasks that require relatively simple geographic tools. These tasks are typically performed on handheld computers (running Microsoft Windows CE or Pocket PC). ArcPad is in wide use today.

- **ArcGIS Desktop and ArcGIS Engine.** These products provide tools for high-end mobile GIS with sophisticated mapping, display, and editing tools. These solutions focus on field tasks that require more sophisticated geographic tools, typically running on high-end Tablet PCs. Often, the map displays used in the field on Tablet PCs must contain detailed information in high-resolution.

- **ArcGIS Mobile Developer Kit included with ArcGIS Server.** Field GIS often relies on custom applications that run on a range of devices (mobile phones, Pocket PCs, and Tablet PCs) and can work in a sometimes-connected mode to GIS servers. These applications often need to be engineered to support the special workflows and tasks for a select group of mobile workers. These applications focus on the field work tasks and the need for productive, simple-to-use interfaces that work well in the field and help to avoid errors in data collection. Often, the ability to send and receive updates from the field is also a key requirement. To support these requirements, ArcGIS Server includes a mobile developer toolkit that is used to build simple, focused mobile applications. These mobile applications can support wireless access to real-time data feeds from central GIS Web servers. ArcGIS Mobile is designed to address these and many other field GIS needs.

ESRI's ArcPad software is mobile GIS technology for Windows mobile devices. ArcPad provides database access, mapping, GIS, and GPS integration to field users via handheld and mobile devices. Data collection with ArcPad is fast and easy and improves field-based data validation and availability.

COMMON ArcPAD FUNCTIONS

- Support for industry-standard vector and raster image display

- ArcIMS client for data access via wireless technology

- Map navigation, including pan and zoom, spatial bookmarks, and center on the current GPS position

- Data query to identify features, display hyperlinks, and locate features

- Map measurement: distance, area, and bearings

- GPS navigation to connect a GPS and let ArcPad guide you

- Simple editing: creating and editing spatial data using input from the mouse pointer, pen, or GPS

- Mobile geodatabase editing: checking out, converting, and projecting GIS data using ArcGIS; editing in the field with ArcPad, and posting changes back to the central GIS database

- Application development to automate GIS fieldwork

ArcPAD APPLICATION BUILDER

Creating a personalized and custom field solution for mapping, data collection, and updates is essential for mobile GIS. ArcPad users are able to customize ArcPad and build focused applications using ArcPad Application Builder.

ArcPad Application Builder runs on Windows computers. Developers build custom applications within this environment and can deploy them on numerous ArcPad devices in their organization.

ArcPad application example: GeoCollector from Trimble and ESRI

Trimble and ESRI have teamed to build a professional GPS solution for field data collection and use called GeoCollector™. This is a complete, out-of-the-box field GIS solution. It includes a mobile device using ArcPad with built-in GPS and application software that supports data collection using GPS field observations. Components in GeoCollector include:

- Trimble® GeoExplorer® handheld device

- ESRI ArcPad software

- Trimble GPScorrect™ extension for ArcPad

- Trimble GPS Analyst extension for ArcGIS Desktop (optional)

GeoCollector has three device options based on accuracy requirements:

- 1–3 meter

- Sub-meter

- Sub-foot

The GeoCollector solution from ESRI and Trimble runs on Trimble's GeoExplorer devices and includes ESRI's ArcPad software.

Many users have requirements for high-end field computers with built-in GPS. These field computers run the full Windows operating system and are used for remotely performing many advanced, computer-based tasks. In recent years, Microsoft has introduced a new operating system, Microsoft Windows XP Tablet PC Edition, which enables many innovative features such as pen-based computing, digital ink technology, and enhanced mobility functions.

ArcGIS Desktop and ArcGIS Engine running on Tablet PCs is a powerful mobile platform for advanced GIS field computing. Tablet PC technology enables users to redline designs, capture accurate field measurements using GPS, and leverage the comprehensive functionality of ArcGIS and the geodatabase in the field.

OVERVIEW OF TABLET PC

A key capability of the Tablet PC is the use of a pen-based interface for computer interaction, sketching, and capturing notes. These activities are based on a technology called digital ink. Digital ink is created through sketching and can be converted to text using the text recognition engine, added to the edit sketch for any editing task, or stored as a graphic in datasets.

The Tablet PC platform is commonly used in four ways:

• Tablet PC as a notebook computer: The Windows XP Tablet PC Edition is a superset of the existing Windows XP operating system.

• Tablet PC pen-based technology: The Tablet PC lets you drive the Windows XP operating system and all Windows-based applications using a digital pen instead of a mouse. For example, in ArcGIS, the digital pen can be used to push buttons on toolbars and draw on the map.

• Windows XP speech recognition: The speech recognition functionality is embedded within the Tablet PC input panel and can be used with ArcGIS for dictation functions.

• Tablet PC digital ink technology: Pen interfaces are used for sketching with Tablet PC's. Digital ink, created through sketching, can be converted to text using the text recognition engine, added to the edit sketch for completion of a current editing task, or stored as a graphic.

ArcGIS DESKTOP AND ENGINE TABLET TOOLS

ArcGIS includes a series of tools for Tablet PCs that enable users to take advantage of its innovative features—pen-based computing, digital ink technology, and enhanced mobility functions as well as the mapping and data compilation capabilities of ArcGIS.

The primary focus is on supporting rich mapping and editing tools for Tablet PCs using ArcGIS Desktop and ArcGIS Engine.

Tablet PC capabilities work very well with ArcGIS Engine. For example, ArcGIS Engine users can apply the pen interface to highlight and query features, create gestures for map navigation and use, add and change attribute values, edit features in the map on Tablet PCs, record map notes, and interact with their custom applications.

ArcGIS Engine application example: GO!Sync MapBook from Tadpole Technology

A good example of an ArcGIS Engine application written for Tablet PCs is Tadpole Technology's GO!Sync™ MapBook application for field use of ArcGIS maps and geodatabases.

Tadpole offers this as a solution product for field data inspection, collection, and redlining. This Tablet PC application enables users to go into the field with sophisticated ArcMap documents and geodatabase contents that support workflows where a highly detailed map that integrates well with GPS locations is needed.

The GO!Sync MapBook application built by Tadpole Technology using ArcGIS Engine

MOBILE SUPPORT IN ArcGIS DESKTOP AND ArcGIS ENGINE

ArcGIS Desktop and ArcGIS Engine support a special Tablet PC toolbar that integrates digital ink technology with ArcGIS. Using the Tablet toolbar, users can access ink tools to create map notes, sketch diagrams, and tie these to geographic locations. The ink tools can also be used to highlight features on a map and sketch shapes and notes that can be used to support GIS editing tasks. Tablet tools make use of ink technology such as gestures and text recognition.

Sketches and notes created in ArcMap on the Tablet PC are geographically referenced and can be saved as map graphics or as annotation features in the geodatabase.

The Tablet tools for ArcGIS add a graphic element called an ink graphic. Ink graphics are stored along with other graphic elements and text in the map's graphics layer or as annotation features in the geodatabase.

Users can create an ink graphic using ArcGIS and choose whether to store the graphic in the map or the geodatabase being edited.

Here is a list of some of the Tablet toolbar functions:

- Pen tool—Creates new ink graphics on the map.

- Highlighter tool—Draws transparent ink on the map for highlighting features.

- Erase tool—Removes strokes of ink from the map display.

- Finish Ink Sketch command—Creates new ink graphic elements from the ink that is being collected on the map.

- Clear Ink Sketch command—Removes all ink that is being collected.

- Add Ink To Sketch command—Allows ink to be used to complete the current editing task (such as creating new features).

- Recognize Ink Graphic command—Converts selected ink graphics written with the Pen tool to text elements.

- Reactivate the Selected Ink Graphic command—Creates a new ink sketch from the selected ink graphic so it can be edited using the Pen or Highlighter tool.

- Find Ink Graphic tool—searches the map or a geodatabase for ink based on its recognized text.

TABLET PC CUSTOMIZATION

Mobile GIS frequently requires focused application designs and customization to build productive, simple user interfaces for field workers. Since ArcGIS is being used, the same customization and ArcObjects programming tasks built with ArcGIS Engine can be leveraged for building and deploying Tablet PC applications.

ArcGIS Server offers a SDK, known as ArcGIS Mobile, that can be used to create and deploy focused mobile applications that operate in a "sometimes connected" environment and can be deployed to a large number of users.

This supports development of custom mobile GIS applications for mobile phones, Pocket PCs, and Tablet PCs.

These applications support mobile mapping, GPS, wireless synchronization, GIS data replication, and editing capabilities on a range of field devices running Microsoft Windows Mobile technology.

Using the ArcGIS Server mobile technology, you can build highly focused mobile GIS applications that you design with a specific field workflow in mind and that synchronize changes directly with the geodatabase while connected in the field. Focused applications require little to no training for the field worker and can use the terminology that is familiar to field workers. You can grow and release new functionality at your own pace based upon user needs and changes to field workflows.

ArcGIS Mobile supports editing against versioned and non-versioned ArcSDE geodatabases using both connected and disconnected workflows. Periodically, you can synchronize updates directly with ArcGIS Server without returning to the office.

ArcGIS Server Mobile runs on a range of mobile devices: Smart Phones, Pocket PCs, and Tablet PCs.

CAPABILITIES INCLUDED IN THE ARCGIS MOBILE SDK

ArcGIS Mobile is designed to build custom applications that work with maps and geodatabases in ArcGIS. The programmer's interface is designed to leverage these capabilities.

The ArcGIS Mobile SDK extends the map service capabilities of ArcGIS Server to enable the distribution of geospatial information to mobile devices. Maps created in ArcMap become part of the mobile map applications that are used in the field.

Mobile maps should be designed so that they contain the map views that are useful for field use. Considerations need to be made when designing these mobile maps—such as the form factor and resolution of the device, map symbology, scale dependencies, and the clarity of the map symbols.

Map cache

Maps that you display and edit on a mobile device are stored in a special high performance mobile map cache. The mobile map cache is a folder of files that stores the mobile map published to ArcGIS Server. It supports both connected and disconnected workflows. Using the mobile map cache, you can connect to ArcGIS Server and synchronize changes.

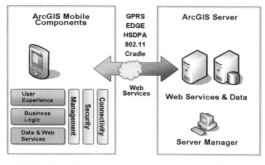

ArcGIS Mobile is a Microsoft Mobile developer toolkit for ArcGIS Server.

Map and map layers

Mobile maps are map documents that are authored using ArcMap and published using ArcGIS Server. They are displayed using a mobile map control. The map control reads from the map cache and displays its contents as a map on the mobile device. This makes it easy to build a mobile map application in Visual Studio.

Example of the embeddable mobile map control used for programming mobile map applications with ArcGIS Mobile. The map control displays the mobile map and includes tools for map interaction and use.

Sketch and geometry

Using the sketch and geometry components, you can quickly build editing tools to create new features and update the shapes of existing features in your mobile map. ArcGIS Mobile includes feature editing tools such as add new features, split features, modify features, snapping, and the use of GPS input for feature coordinates.

GPS integration

Most mobile applications integrate GPS locations either as a navigational aid or as input to the creation and update of features.

Day-to-day synchronization

Once you have deployed your application, your field workers can synchronize the data updates that they make in the field as well as receive map updates made by others to update their mobile maps.

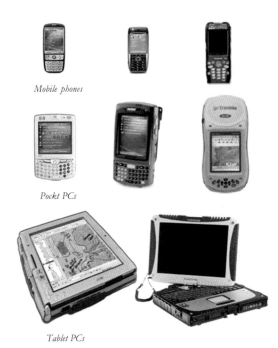

Mobile phones

Pocket PCs

Tablet PCs

ArcGIS Mobile works across a range of field devices.

7

GIS data concepts, the geodatabase, and ArcSDE

A cornerstone of ArcGIS is its ability to access GIS data in any format and use multiple databases, file-based datasets, DBMS tables, and GIS Web services. Generally, most external data sources are used as feature classes or attribute tables or as raster data sources within ArcGIS.

ArcGIS supports direct use of a number of GIS and tabular data formats. ArcGIS also includes a series of geoprocessing tools for data conversion that can be used to transfer data between supported formats such as the geodatabase.

Feature data sources
ESRI coverages
ESRI shapefiles
Vector product format (VPF)
CAD data sources (numerous formats)
NetCDF
GML

Raster data sources
ESRI GRID
ERDAS Imagine
TIFF and Geo TIFF
JPEG and JPEG 2000
CADRG
HDF
MrSID
ER Mapper

Geodatabase
Personal geodatabases (in Microsoft Access)
File geodatabases (native file systems)
Oracle
Oracle with Spatial or Locator
SQL Server
IBM DB2
Informix
Geodatabase XML

Some of the common GIS data sources used directly in ArcGIS. Access to and from numerous additional formats is supported. Many more formats are also available using the optional ArcGIS Data Interoperability extension. GIS data is also accessible through the Web using various XML and Web schemas, such as Geodatabase XML, ArcXML, SOAP, and KML; and using OGC specifications, such as WMS, GML, and WFS.

Support for file-based models includes access to numerous GIS datasets such as coverages, shapefiles, grids, images, and TINs. The geodatabase model manages the same types of geographic information in relational databases and file systems, providing many of the data management benefits offered by a DBMS.

Both the file-based datasets and the DBMS-based datasets define a generic model for geographic information. This generic model can be used to define and work with a wide variety of GIS applications. By defining and implementing the behavior of a generic geographic data model, geographic information in ArcGIS can be multipurpose, sharable, and standards-based. Most important, a comprehensive series of tools are available to work with the generic data types. ArcGIS provides a robust platform for virtually any GIS application.

In addition, ESRI and Safe Software have integrated the Safe Software FME product into ArcGIS—the optional ArcGIS Data Interoperability extension. This adds support for dozens of additional data formats that can be used directly within ArcGIS as well as the ability to define new custom data sources and data transformation procedures that allow advanced data transformations between a variety of GIS and tabular data structures.

The geodatabase is the native data structure for ArcGIS and is the primary data format used for editing and data management.

The geodatabase is a collection of geographic datasets of various types held in a common file system folder, a Microsoft Access database, or a multiuser relational database (such as Oracle, Microsoft SQL Server, or IBM DB2).

Geodatabases work across a range of DBMS architectures and file systems, come in many sizes, and have varying numbers of users. They can scale from small, single-user databases built on files up to larger workgroup, department, and enterprise geodatabases accessed by many users.

ADVANCED GEOGRAPHIC DATA TYPES EXTEND FEATURE CLASSES, RASTERS, AND ATTRIBUTE TABLES

The three most common dataset types in the geodatabase are feature classes, raster datasets, and attribute tables. Creating a collection of these dataset types provides the first step in designing and building a geodatabase. Users typically start by building a number of these fundamental dataset types. Then, they add to or extend their geodatabase with more advanced capabilities (such as adding topologies, networks, terrains, relationships, and subtypes). These extended data types are critical in most GIS applications in order to model rich GIS behavior, maintain data integrity, and work with important sets of spatial relationships.

A series of advanced geodatabase types are used to extend simple tables, features, and rasters. These include properties for coordinate systems, coordinate resolution, feature classes, topologies, networks, raster catalogs, relationships, domains, cartographic representations, address locators, and so forth. The geodatabase schema includes the definitions, integrity rules, and behavior for each of these extended capabilities.

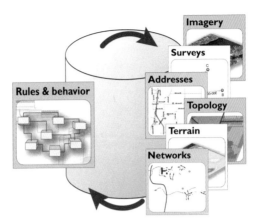

Geodatabases support a number of rich geographic data types that are used to add GIS behavior, maintain data integrity, and access critical spatial relationships between features.

TYPES OF GEODATABASES

There are three types of geodatabases:

1. File geodatabases—Stored as folders in a file system. There is no limit on the geodatabase size. Each dataset is held as a file that can scale up to 1TB in size. This limit can be extended to 256TB for very large raster datasets. The file geodatabase supports one editor and many readers (as many users as file systems can typically handle before performance degrades). Long transactions and versioning are not supported.

2. Personal geodatabases— All datasets are stored within a Microsoft Access data file, which is limited in size to 2GB. However, the effective limit before performance degrades is typically between 250 and 500MB per Access database file. A personal geodatabase is not as fast, efficient, or scalable as file geodatabases; however, it supports attribute manipulation and string handling in Microsoft Access. Long transactions and versioning are not supported.

3. ArcSDE geodatabases—Stored in a relational database such as Oracle, Microsoft SQL Server, IBM DB2, or IBM Informix. ArcSDE geodatabases support multiple users and editors and support long transactions in GIS-using versioning. These multiuser geodatabases require ArcSDE technology, which is included in ArcGIS Desktop and ArcGIS Server. In ArcSDE geodatabases, there is no limit to size or numbers of users.

ArcSDE is ESRI's technology for accessing and managing geospatial data within relational databases. ArcSDE technology supports reading and writing of multiple standards, including (among other data storage options) OGC for simple features, the ISO standard for spatial types, and the Oracle Spatial format. At ArcGIS 9.2, ArcSDE technology is being enhanced to support non-versioned editing and full SQL access to geodatabases managed within Oracle DBMSs.

ArcSDE is unique in its support of the following capabilities:

- It is open and interoperable across multiple DBMSs (Oracle, SQL Server, DB2, and Informix).

- It is standards-based, using as its native data structure the OGC binary simple features standard and the ISO spatial type (for Oracle, IBM DB2, and Informix only). At ArcGIS 9.2, support for the ISO-type standard has been added to the Oracle platform.

- It supports full, open SQL access to geodatabases stored in Oracle, IBM DB2, and Informix.

- It fully supports the Oracle format for feature storage (using Oracle Spatial and Oracle Locator).

- It provides high performance and scales to a large number of users. ArcSDE geodatabases outperform all other solutions for storage and retrieval of spatial data.

WHEN DO YOU NEED ArcSDE?

When you need a large multiuser geodatabase that can be edited and used simultaneously by many users, the ArcSDE geodatabase provides the solution. It adds the ability to manage both a shared, multiuser geodatabase and a number of critical version-based GIS workflows. The ability to leverage an organization's enterprise relational databases is a key advantage of the ArcSDE geodatabase.

ArcSDE also supports users who need to manage long transactions and versioned-based workflows—for example, to manage historical archives, distributed editing, federated replicas managed across many DBMS architectures, and to support multiuser editing scenarios.

ArcSDE geodatabases work with a variety of DBMS storage models (IBM DB2, Informix, Oracle, and SQL Server). ArcSDE geodatabases are used in a wide range of work groups, departments, and enterprise settings. They take full advantage of their underlying DBMS architectures to support:

- Extremely large, continuous GIS databases

- Many simultaneous users

- Long transactions and versioned workflows

- Relational database support for GIS data management (providing the benefits of a relational database such as scalability, reliability, security, backup, and integrity)

- Standards-based SQL Types for Spatial when the DBMS supports this capability (Oracle, Informix, and IBM DB2).

Through many large geodatabase implementations, it has been found that DBMSs are efficient at moving the type of large binary objects required for GIS data in and out of tables. In addition, GIS database sizes and the number of supported users can be much larger using ArcSDE.

In the past, ArcSDE was sold as a separate ESRI product. At ArcGIS 9.2, ArcSDE technology is still included in ArcGIS; however, it is no longer a separate product. Instead, ArcSDE technology has been integrated into both the ArcGIS Server and ArcGIS Desktop products.

ArcSDE geodatabases readily scale from personal, singleuser geodatabases, through workgroup geodatabases, on up to extremely large enterprise geodatabases.

There are three levels for accessing and using ArcSDE technology in ArcGIS. Geodatabase capabilities are available in the following ESRI software:

	Personal ArcSDE	Workgroup ArcSDE	Enterprise ArcSDE
ArcGIS Product	Included with ArcEditor and ArcInfo	Included with ArcGIS Sever Workgroup	Included with ArcGIS Server Enterprise
Number of ArcSDE geodatabase users	Max.3 users and 1 editor at any time	Max. 10 clients at any time No limit on the number of connections from servers	Unlimited
Supported DBMSs	SQL Server Express 1GB RAM 1 CPU	SQL Server Express 1GB RAM 1 CPU	SQL Server Oracle IBM DB2 Informix
Database size limits	Max database size 4GB	Max database size 4GB	No limits

PERSONAL ArcSDE TECHNOLOGY INCLUDED WITH ArcEDITOR AND ArcINFO

Beginning at ArcGIS 9.2, ArcEditor and ArcInfo include the Microsoft SQL Server Express database free of charge. These software products also include ArcSDE capabilities to support personal ArcSDE geodatabases for three simultaneous users—one of whom can edit data.

SQL Server Express is limited to only use 1 CPU (or Core within a Socket) and utilize 1GB RAM. The maximum database size for SQL Server Express is 4GB.

Within ArcEditor and ArcInfo, the ArcCatalog application provides the ability to fully administer and manage ArcSDE geodatabases using SQL Server Express. This provides full ArcSDE geodatabase capabilities for a few users and one editor at a time. You set up and manage these ArcSDE geodatabases within ArcCatalog. No extra software or database administration expertise is required.

WORKGROUP ArcSDE TECHNOLOGY INCLUDED WITH ArcGIS SERVER WORKGROUP

ArcGIS Server Workgroup includes ArcSDE support for SQL Server Express. With this level of ArcSDE, you can use SQL Server Express for up to 10 simultaneous Windows desktop users and editors (for example, users of ArcView, ArcEditor, ArcInfo, a custom ArcGIS Engine application, AutoCAD, MicroStation, and so on) plus any number of additional server connections that can be supported by your configuration.

SQL Server Express is limited to only use 1 CPU (or Core) and utilize 1GB RAM. Maximum database size is 4GB.

As with personal ArcSDE, you can use ArcEditor or ArcInfo to create, administer, and manage workgroup ArcSDE geodatabases. You set up and manage these workgroup ArcSDE geodatabases using SQL Server Express within ArcCatalog. No extra database administration expertise is required.

In this context, you can think of ArcGIS Server Workgroup as an extension for ArcEditor or ArcInfo to help you manage and serve workgroup ArcSDE geodatabases. Of course, ArcGIS Server can perform many more functions and tasks.

ENTERPRISE ArcSDE TECHNOLOGY INCLUDED WITH ArcGIS SERVER ENTERPRISE

This is the traditional ArcSDE technology that runs on Oracle, SQL Server, IBM DB2, and IBM Informix and can scale to databases of any size and number of users, running on computers of any size and configuration. Users provide their own DBMS license for this level of ArcSDE use. The DBMS is typically administered and managed by a database administrator (DBA).

ONE SCALABLE GEODATA ARCHITECTURE

These various support levels for ArcSDE enable users to take full advantage of ArcSDE geodatabases for any number of users—large or small. It allows organizations to have one scalable data architecture that works across their single user systems up to their large enterprise systems.

Feature classes are homogeneous collections of common features, each having the same spatial representation, such as a point, line, or polygon, and a common set of attribute columns—for example, a line feature class representing road centerlines. The four most commonly used feature classes in the geodatabase are Points, Lines, Polygons, and Annotation (which is the geodatabase name for map text).

MODELING FEATURE BEHAVIOR

In the illustration below, there are four feature classes for the same area: parcel polygons, sewer lines, manhole cover locations as points, and street name annotation.

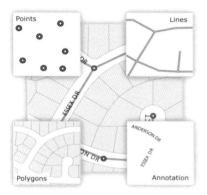

Four feature classes that represent parcels, sewer lines, manhole covers, and street name annotation.

In this diagram, there is also the potential requirement to model some advanced feature properties. For example, the sewer lines and manhole locations make up a storm sewer network—a system with which you can model runoff and flows. Also, adjacent parcels share common boundaries. Most parcel users want to maintain the integrity of shared feature boundaries in their datasets using a topology.

Most users need to model such spatial relationships and behaviors in their geographic datasets. In these cases, users will extend these basic feature classes by adding a number of advanced geodatabase elements such as topologies, network datasets, terrains, address locators, and so forth.

FEATURE GEOMETRY

Feature geometry is primarily composed of coordinate vertices and segments between vertices (in line and polygon features). Segments are the two-point edges that are used to represent the shape of boundaries. Segments are most typically straight edges, but they can also be parametrically defined curves.

Vertices in features can also include z values to represent elevation measures and m values to represent measurements along line features.

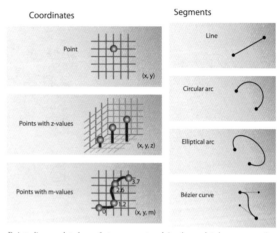

Point, line, and polygon features are stored in the geodatabase as a series of vertices whose locations are recorded using xy coordinates. Vertices can also have z values for representing elevation and m values for locating measures along lines (for example, in distance or time units). The shape of a feature between two vertices is defined by a segment. Typically, these are simple straight-line segments. However, some feature segments can be represented as curves, as illustrated above.

Rasters are used to represent continuous layers, such as elevation, slope and aspect, vegetation, temperature, rainfall, plume dispersion, and so on. Rasters are most commonly used for the storage of aerial photographs and imagery of various kinds.

In addition to vector features and raster datasets, other spatial data types can be managed and stored in the geodatabase, allowing users the opportunity to manage all geographic data types using the geodatabase.

Raster datasets are the storage mechanisms for imagery data.

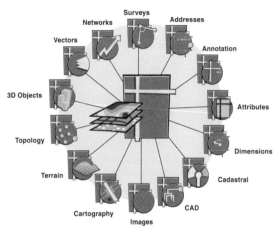

Geodatabases are used to manage and store diverse collections of geographic information types.

Users usually think of the geodatabase as a physical store of their geographic information—primarily using a DBMS or file system. In addition to being a physical instance of a collection of datasets, each geodatabase has some key additional aspects:

• Geodatabases have a comprehensive information model for representing and managing geographic information. This comprehensive information model is implemented as a series of simple data tables holding feature classes, raster datasets, and attributes. In addition, advanced GIS data objects add GIS behavior, rules for managing spatial integrity, and tools for working with numerous spatial relationships of the core features, rasters, and attributes.

• Geodatabase software logic provides the common application logic used throughout ArcGIS for accessing and working with geographic data in a variety of files and formats. This logic is also used to work with shapefiles, CAD files, TINs, grids, imagery, and numerous other GIS data sources.

• Geodatabases have a transaction model for managing GIS data workflows.

Each of these aspects of the geodatabase is described in detail in the sections that follow.

Users tend to think of the relational DBMS as inherently open because the simplicity and flexibility of the generic relational data model enable it to support a broad array of applications.

The geodatabase storage model is based on these DBMS principles—leveraging a series of simple, yet essential, relational database concepts. The DBMS (and the file system for file geodatabases) provides a simple, formal data model for storing and working with information in tables.

KEY CONCEPTS

- Data is organized into tables.

- Tables contain rows.

- All rows in a table have the same columns.

- Each column has a type, such as integer, decimal number, character, date, and so on.

- Relationships are used to associate rows from one table with rows in another table. This is based on a common column in each table.

- Relational integrity rules exist for tables. For example, each row always shares the same columns, a domain lists the valid values or value ranges for a column, and so on.

For ArcSDE geodatabases that are held in relational databases, a number of additional DBMS capabilities also apply:

- SQL, a series of relational functions and operators, is available to operate on the tables and their data elements.

- The SQL operators are designed to work with the generic relational data types, such as integers, decimal numbers, dates, and characters.

For example, a feature class is stored as a DBMS table. Each row represents a feature. The columns in each row represent various characteristics or properties of the feature, and one of the columns holds the feature geometry (for example, point, line, or polygon coordinates). In the example above, the shape field holds a polygon shape for each parcel row in the feature class table.

Feature class table

Shape	ID	PIN	Area	Addr	Code
	1	334-1626-001	7,342	341 Cherry Ct.	SFR
	2	334-1626-002	8,020	343 Cherry Ct.	UND
	3	334-1626-003	10,031	345 Cherry Ct.	SFR
	4	334-1626-004	9,254	347 Cherry Ct.	SFR
	5	334-1626-005	8,856	348 Cherry Ct.	UND
	6	334-1626-006	9,975	346 Cherry Ct.	SFR
	7	334-1626-007	8,230	344 Cherry Ct.	SFR
	8	334-1626-008	8,645	342 Cherry Ct.	SFR

Related ownership table

PIN	Owner	Acq.Date	Assessed	TaxStat
334-1626-001	G. Hall	1995/10/20	$115,500.00	02
334-1626-002	H. L Holmes	1993/10/06	$24,375.00	01
334-1626-003	W. Rodgers	1980/09/24	$175,500.00	02
334-1626-004	J. Williamson	1974/09/20	$135,750.00	02
334-1626-005	P. Goodman	1966/06/06	$30,350.00	02
334-1626-006	K. Staley	1942/10/24	$120,750.00	02
334-1626-007	J. Dormandy	1996/01/27	$110,650.00	01
334-1626-008	S. Gooley	2000/05/31	$145,750.00	02

Various column types in the DBMS are used to hold the shape field in the table. These are typically either a binary large object (BLOB) type or an extended spatial type that is supported in some DBMSs. For example, ESRI provides a spatial column type for storing features in ArcSDE geodatabases managed in Oracle, IBM DB2, and Informix.

SQL operates on the rows, columns, and types in tables. The column types (the numbers, characters, dates, BLOBs, spatial types, and so on) are objects in the SQL algebra. The DBMS manages these simple data types and tables, while additional application logic implements more complex object behavior and integrity constraints.

IMPLEMENTING HIGHER LEVEL OBJECTS AND BEHAVIOR IN RELATIONAL DBMSs

Developers wanting to implement higher-level objects with behavior and logic write application code to do so. For example, an organization may implement a table named EMPLOYEES as follows:

Name (Last)	Name (First)	DOH	Salary
Crosier	James	10-10-98	10,000.75
Clark	Rosemary	03-12-95	55,000.50
Brown	Pete	06-12-89	23,000.00

A simple relational data table containing rows and columns. The data in each column adheres to a particular data type, such as character, date, and number.

The table above is a simple relational data table containing rows and columns. The data in each column adheres to a particular SQL data type, such as character, date, and number. DBMSs work with information at this SQL type level.

However, simply adding this information to a DBMS table does not turn the DBMS into a payroll or employee management system. Adding a column named "Dollars" that holds numbers with two decimal places does not turn a DBMS into an accounting system. Higher level application logic is needed.

Examples of logic that could be implemented to support employment activities are hiring, implementing a pay raise, employee resignations, promotions, and managing benefits. The business objects being modeled for the employees and their names, salaries, and hire dates are not implemented as relational objects. More sophisticated and focused application logic is required to implement behavior and integrity on these business objects.

Similar business objects are universally applied in GIS. For example, topologies, networks, linear referencing systems, raster catalogs, annotations, terrains, map layers, and so forth are all examples of advanced objects used to implement GIS behavior on top of the simple spatial representations stored in the DBMS.

As with other DBMS applications, tables with spatial column types are not enough on their own for GIS applications. Both sets of objects (the simple DBMS relational column types and the geodatabase application objects such as topologies) are necessary for building geographic information systems.

Where does the application logic belong?

Various alternatives exist. Users can persist this higher-level logic in a number of ways. For example, the logic could be implemented as:

- Stored procedures and database triggers in the DBMS

- Extended types in the DBMS

- A separate application tier that works on the rows and column types in tables

Countless DBMS implementations over the past two decades have demonstrated overwhelmingly that the use of an application tier is appropriate for advanced applications. For example, all the widely adopted customer information systems (CIS), enterprise resource planning (ERP) systems, and accounting packages implement advanced application logic in the application tier, which enables more openness and extensibility, higher performance, richer toolsets, scalability, and increased flexibility.

Users interact with and perform transactions within these systems through the application logic for the vast majority of operations and only leverage SQL for focused (and appropriate) activities.

Separating the application logic above the data tier also allows the same logic to be applied to DBMSs, files, XML, and other data storage alternatives. This enables this architecture to be more open. For example, the geodatabase application logic in ArcGIS is also used to read and work with all geographic data sources—CAD data, shapefiles, MapInfo data, Intergraph® GeoMedia® files, GML profiles, and so forth.

The geodatabase employs a multitier application architecture by implementing advanced logic and behavior in the application tier on top of the data storage tier (managed within DBMSs, files, or XML). The geodatabase application logic includes support for a series of generic GIS data objects and behaviors such as feature classes, raster datasets, topologies, networks, and address locators, among others.

This multitier geodatabase architecture is sometimes referred to as an object-relational model.

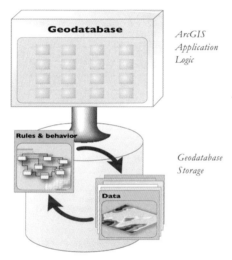

The geodatabase architecture is based on simple relational storage and comprehensive application logic.

Responsibility for management of geographic datasets is shared between ArcGIS software and the generic DBMS. Certain aspects of geographic dataset management, such as disk-based storage, definition of attribute types, associative query processing, and multiuser transaction processing, are delegated to the DBMS. The GIS application retains responsibility for defining the specific DBMS schema used to represent various geographic datasets and for domain-specific logic, which maintains the integrity and utility of the underlying records.

In effect, the DBMS is used as one of a series of implementation mechanisms for persisting geographic datasets. However, the DBMS does not fully define the semantics of the geographic data. This could be considered a multitier architecture (application and

storage), where aspects related to data storage and retrieval are implemented in the data storage (DBMS) tier as simple tables, while high-level data integrity, management of spatial relationships, geographic behavior, and information processing functions are retained in the application and domain software (ArcGIS).

The geodatabase is implemented using the same multitier application architecture found in other advanced DBMS applications. The geodatabase objects are persisted as rows in DBMS tables that have identity, and the behavior is supplied through the geodatabase application logic.

All ArcGIS applications interact with this generic GIS object model for geodatabases, not with the actual SQL-based DBMS instance. The geodatabase software components implement behavior and integrity rules implicit in the generic model and translate data requests to the appropriate physical database design. ArcSDE software provides a gateway for ArcGIS to interact with the DBMS.

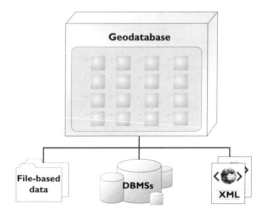

The separation of geodatabase logic from storage enables support for numerous file types, DBMSs, and XML.

The separation of geodatabase logic from storage enables open support for numerous file types, DBMSs, and XML. For example, the capability to access almost any feature and tabular data format is provided by the ArcGIS Data Interoperability extension. This extension provides a gateway to read and work with dozens of data formats using geodatabase logic.

At the core of the geodatabase is a standard relational database schema (a series of standard DBMS tables, column types, indexes, and so on). This simple physical storage works in concert with, and is controlled by, a set of higher-level application objects hosted in the application tier, which can be an ArcGIS desktop, embedded ArcGIS engine logic, or an ArcGIS server.

Each of these includes geodatabase objects that define a generic GIS information model that is shared by all ArcGIS applications and users. The purpose of the geodatabase objects is to expose a high-level GIS information model to clients and to persist the detailed implementation of this model in any appropriate storage model—for example, in standard DBMS tables, in file geodatabases, and as XML streams.

Geodatabase storage includes both the schema and rule base for each geographic dataset plus simple, tabular storage of the spatial and attribute data.

The geodatabase schema includes the definitions, integrity rules, and behavior for each geographic dataset. These include properties for feature classes, topologies, networks, raster catalogs, relationships, domains, and so forth. The schema is persisted in a collection of geodatabase metatables in the DBMS that defines the integrity and behavior of the geographic information.

The spatial representations are most commonly stored as either vector features or as raster datasets along with traditional tabular attributes. For example, a DBMS table can be used to store a feature class where each row in the table represents a feature. A shape column in each row is used to hold the geometry or shape of the feature. The shape column holding the geometry is typically one of two column types:

- A spatial column type, if the DBMS supports it

- A binary large object (BLOB) column type

A homogeneous collection of common features, each having the same spatial representation, such as a point, line, or polygon, and a common set of attribute columns, is referred to as a feature class and is managed in a single table.

Raster and imagery data types are managed and stored in relational tables as well. Raster data is typically much larger in size and requires a side table for storage. The raster is tiled into smaller pieces, or blocks, and each

block is stored in individual rows in the separate block table.

The column types that hold the vector and raster geometry vary from database to database. When the DBMS supports spatial type extensions, the geodatabase can readily use them to hold the spatial geometry.

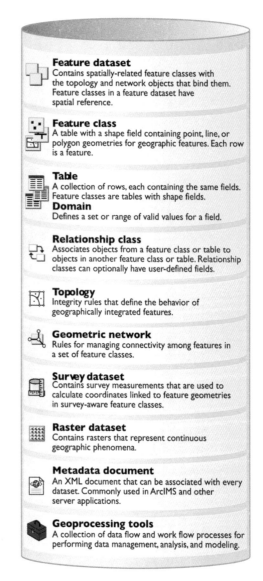

Feature dataset
Contains spatially-related feature classes with the topology and network objects that bind them. Feature classes in a feature dataset have spatial reference.

Feature class
A table with a shape field containing point, line, or polygon geometries for geographic features. Each row is a feature.

Table
A collection of rows, each containing the same fields. Feature classes are tables with shape fields.

Domain
Defines a set or range of valid values for a field.

Relationship class
Associates objects from a feature class or table to objects in another feature class or table. Relationship classes can optionally have user-defined fields.

Topology
Integrity rules that define the behavior of geographically integrated features.

Geometric network
Rules for managing connectivity among features in a set of feature classes.

Survey dataset
Contains survey measurements that are used to calculate coordinates linked to feature geometries in survey-aware feature classes.

Raster dataset
Contains rasters that represent continuous geographic phenomena.

Metadata document
An XML document that can be associated with every dataset. Commonly used in ArcIMS and other server applications.

Geoprocessing tools
A collection of data flow and work flow processes for performing data management, analysis, and modeling.

Some of the common data types in the geodatabase used to develop a rich, geographic information model.

Transactions are packages of work that make changes to databases. GIS databases, like other database applications, must support update transactions that enforce data integrity and application behavior. In many cases, users can exploit the DBMS's transaction framework for managing edits and updates to geodatabases.

However, GIS users universally have specialized transactional requirements, the most important of which is that transactions must span long periods of time (sometimes days and months, not just seconds or minutes).

Additionally, most GIS editing involves orchestrating changes to multiple rows in multiple tables and managing these as a single unified transaction.. Users need to be able to undo and redo changes. Editing sessions can span several hours or even days. Often the edits must be performed in a system that is disconnected from the central, shared database.

Because GIS workflow processes may span days or months, the GIS database must remain continuously available for daily operations, where each user might have a personal view or state of the shared GIS database. In a multiuser database, the GIS transactions must be managed on the DBMS's short transaction framework. ArcSDE plays a key role during these operations by managing the high-level, complex GIS transactions on the simple DBMS transaction framework.

GIS users have many cases in which long transaction workflows are critical. In most instances, these are made possible through the use of a multiuser DBMS and ArcSDE to manage updates to the central GIS database.

The following are examples of GIS data compilation workflows that require a long transaction model:

- **Multiple edit sessions**—A single GIS database update may require numerous changes that span multiple edit sessions occurring over a few days or weeks.

- **Multiuser editing**—Multiple editors often need to concurrently update the same spatially integrated features. Each user needs to work with a personalized database state, viewing individual updates and ignoring updates by other editors. Eventually, each user needs to post and reconcile their updates with the other editors to identify and resolve any conflicts.

- **Checkout/check-in transactions**—It's often necessary to check out a portion of a database for a particular area or district to a personal computer or mobile device and update that information in a disconnected session that could last for days or weeks. These updates must be posted to the main database.

- **History**—Sometimes it's advantageous to maintain a historical version of each feature in a GIS database, even after that particular version has been updated, to maintain a copy of the retired and changed features in an archive or to track an individual feature's history—for example, parcel lineage or feature update properties in a national mapping database.

- **Transfer of change-only updates**—Enterprise databases and spatial data infrastructures in which information is shared across a range of organizations are collaborate efforts that require the sharing of updates across the Internet in a well-defined XML schema for sharing change-only updates between databases.

- **Distributed geographic database replicas**—A regional database may be a partial copy of a main corporate GIS database for a particular geographic region. Periodically, the two databases must be synchronized by exchanging updates.

- **Federated replication across DBMSs**—Often, GIS data must be synchronized among a series of database copies (replicas), where each site performs its own updates on its local database. Often the databases are only periodically connected via the Web. On a scheduled basis, the updates must be transferred from each database replica to the others and their contents synchronized. Many times the DBMSs are different—for example, replicating datasets between SQL Server, Oracle, and IBM DB2.

THE GEODATABASE TRANSACTION MODEL—VERSIONING

The geodatabase mechanism for managing these and many other critical GIS workflows is to maintain multiple states in the geodatabase and, most important, do so while ensuring the integrity of the geographic information, rules, and behavior. This ability to manage, work with, and view multiple states is based on versioning. As the name implies, versioning explicitly records versions of individual features and objects as they are modified, added, and retired through various states. Each version explicitly records each state of a feature or object as a row in a table along with important transaction information. Any number of users can simultaneously work with and manage multiple versions.

Versions enable all transactions to be recorded as a series of changes to the database through time. This means that various users can work with multiple views or states of the geodatabase. The goal is open, high performance multiuser access. For example, the system must be fast and must productively support the use of datasets containing hundreds of millions of records that are being accessed and updated by hundreds of simultaneous users.

ArcSDE technology is used to manage long transactions by leveraging each DBMS's short transaction framework.

Versions explicitly record the object states of a geodatabase in two delta tables: the Adds table and the Deletes table. Simple queries are used to view and work with any state of the geodatabase—for example, to view the database state for a point in time or to see a particular user's current version with edits.

In the example below, a parcel (number 45) is updated and becomes new parcel number 47. Using versioning, the original parcel 45 is saved in the Deletes table and the new parcel 47 in the Adds table. Other metatables record transaction information such as the time and sequence of each update, the version name, and the state IDs.

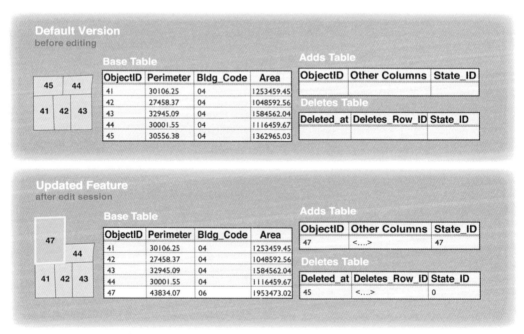

Versions explicitly record the object states of a geodatabase.

Geodatabase XML represents ESRI's open mechanism for information interchange between geodatabases and other external systems. ESRI openly publishes and maintains the complete geodatabase schema and content as an XML specification and provides example implementations to illustrate how users can share data updates between heterogeneous systems.

XML interchange of geospatial information to and from the geodatabase is greatly simplified using the geodatabase XML specification. External applications can receive XML data streams including:

- Exchange and sharing of full or partial geodatabase schemas between ArcGIS users

- Exchange of complete lossless datasets

- Interchange of simple feature sets (much like shapefile interchange)

- Exchange of change-only (delta) record sets using XML streams to pass updates and changes among geodatabases and other external data structures

Geodatabase XML is the primary interchange mechanism for data sharing among ArcGIS users as well as external users.

Glossary

3D multipatch

See multipatch.

address geocoding

See geocoding.

analysis

The process of identifying a question or issue to be addressed, modeling the issue, investigating model results, interpreting the results, and possibly making a recommendation.

annotation

1. In ArcGIS, text or graphics on a map that can be individually selected, positioned, and modified by the software user. The text may represent either feature attributes or supplementary information. Annotation may be manually entered by the user or generated from labels. Annotation is stored either in a map document as text or graphic elements, or in a geodatabase as a feature class.

2. A feature class type in the geodatabase.

ArcIMS

ESRI software that allows for centrally hosting and serving GIS maps, data, and mapping applications as Web services. The administrative framework allows users to author configuration files, publish services, design Web pages, and administer ArcIMS Spatial Servers. ArcIMS supports Windows, Linux, and UNIX platforms and is customizable on many levels.

ArcSDE

Software technology in ArcGIS that provides a gateway for storing, managing, and using spatial data in one of the following commercial database management systems: IBM DB2 UDB, IBM Informix, Microsoft SQL Server, and Oracle. Common ArcSDE client applications include ArcGIS Desktop, ArcGIS Server, ArcGIS Engine, and ArcIMS.

ArcToolbox

A user interface in ArcGIS used for accessing and organizing a collection of geoprocessing tools, models, and scripts. ArcToolbox and ModelBuilder are used in concert to perform geoprocessing.

attribute

1. Information about a geographic feature in a GIS, usually stored in a table and linked to the feature by a unique identifier. For example, attributes of a river might include its name, length, and average depth.

2. In raster datasets, information associated with each unique value of raster cells.

3. Cartographic information that specifies how features are displayed and labeled on a map; the cartographic attributes of a river might include line thickness, line length, color, and font.

attribute key

See primary key.

CAD

See computer-aided drafting (CAD).

CAD dataset

A CAD drawing file that contains graphical elements and drawing attributes. ArcGIS supports many CAD formats including DWG (AutoCAD), DXF (AutoDesk Drawing Exchange Format), and DGN (the default MicroStation file format).

cartography

The art, science, and knowledge of expressing graphically, usually through maps, the natural and social features of the earth.

check-in

The procedure that transfers a copy of data into a master geodatabase, overwriting the original copy of that data and enabling it so it can be accessed and saved from that location.

checkout

The procedure that records the duplication of data from one geodatabase to another and disables the original data so that both versions cannot be accessed or saved at the same time.

checkout geodatabase

Any geodatabase that contains data checked out from a master geodatabase.

checkout version

The data version created in a checkout geodatabase when data is checked out to that database. This version is created as a copy of the synchronization version. Only the edits made to this checkout version can be checked back in to the master geodatabase.

computer-aided drafting (CAD)

A system for the design, drafting, and display of graphically oriented information often used in architecture, engineering, and manufacturing. Also known as computer-aided design.

coverage

A data model for storing geographic features using ArcInfo Workstation. A coverage stores a set of thematically associated data considered to be a unit. It usually represents a single layer, such as soils, streams, roads, or land use. In a coverage, features are stored as both primary features (points, arcs, polygons) and secondary features (tics, links, annotation). Feature attributes are described and stored independently in feature attribute tables.

data

Any collection of related facts arranged in a particular format; often, the basic elements of information that are produced, stored, or processed by a computer.

database management system (DBMS)

A set of computer programs that organizes the information in a database according to a conceptual schema and provides tools for data input, verification, storage, modification, and retrieval.

data model

1. In GIS, a mathematical paradigm for representing geographic objects or surfaces as data. The vector data model represents geography as collections of points, lines, and polygons; the raster data model represents geography as cell matrixes that store numeric values; the TIN data model represents geography as sets of contiguous, non-overlapping triangles.

2. In ArcGIS, a set of database design specifications for objects in a GIS application. A data model describes the thematic layers used in the application (for example, counties, roads, and hamburger stands); their spatial representation (for example, point, line, or polygon); their attributes; their integrity rules and relationships (for example, streets cannot self-intersect, or counties must nest within states); their cartographic portrayal; and their metadata requirements.

3. In information theory, a description of the rules by which data is defined, organized, queried, and updated within an information system (usually a database management software program).

dataset

Any organized collection of data with a common theme.

DBMS

See database management system (DBMS).

DEM

See digital elevation model (DEM).

digital elevation model (DEM)

The representation of continuous elevation values over a topographic surface by a regular array of z-values, referenced to a common data. Typically used to represent terrain relief.

digital terrain model (DTM)

See digital elevation model (DEM).

disconnected editing

The process of copying data from another geodatabase (usually a subset of the data), editing that data, then merging the changes back into the source or master geodatabase.

domain

In geodatabases, the set of valid valaues or ranges of values for an attribute field.

enterprise geodatabase

A centralized geographic database (often managed using a series of federated or distributed copies) that supports an organization's objectives and goals. Enterprise geodatabases are typically multiuser and transactional and are managed in a DBMS using ArcSDE.

enterprise GIS

An integrated, multi-departmental system for collecting, organizing, analyzing, visualizing, managing, and disseminating geographic information. It is intended to address both the collective and the individual needs of an organization, and to make geographic information and services available to GIS and non-GIS professionals.

eXtensible Markup Language (XML)

Developed by the World Wide Web Consortium (W3C), XML is a standard for designing text formats that facilitates the interchange of data between computer applications (for example, across the Web). XML is a set of rules for creating standard information formats using customized tags and sharing both the format and the data across applications.

feature class

A collection of geographic features with the same geometry type (such as point, line, or polygon), the same attribute fields, and the same spatial reference. Feature classes can stand alone within a geodatabase or be contained within a feature dataset. Feature classes allow homogeneous features to be grouped into a single unit for data storage and use. For example, highways, primary roads, and secondary roads can be grouped into a line feature class named roads. In a geodatabase, there are seven feature class types: Point, Line, Polygon, Annotation, Mutlipoints (to hold LIDAR and bathymetry observations), Multipatches (to hold 3D shapes), and Dimensions (a specialize type of annotation). External GIS datasets such as CAD files, OGC GML files, and MapInfo files are accessed as feature classes in ArcGIS.

feature dataset

A collection of related feature classes stored together that share the same spatial reference; that is, they have the same coordinate system. Feature datasets are used to organize feature classes that participate together in a topology, a network, or a terrain dataset.

GDB

See geodatabase (GDB).

geocoding

The process of finding the location of a street address on a map. The location can be an x,y coordinate or a feature such as a street segment, postal delivery location, or building. In GIS, geocoding requires a reference dataset that contains address attributes for the geographic features in the area of interest. The geodatabase contains a data type to support geocoding called an Address Locator.

geodatabase (GDB)

A collection of geographic datasets of various types held in a common file system folder, a Microsoft Access database file, or in a multiuser relational database (such as Oracle, Microsoft SQL Server, IBM DB2, or Informix). The geodatabase is the native data structure used in ArcGIS and is the primary format used for editing and data management.

geodatabase data model

The schema for the various geographic datasets and tables in an instance of a geodatabase. The schema defines the GIS objects, rules, and relationships used to add GIS behavior and integrity to the datasets in a collection.

geodataset

Any GIS-based dataset.

geographic data

Information about real-world features, including their shapes, locations, and descriptions. Geographic data is the composite of spatial data and attribute data.

geographic database

See geodatabase (GDB).

geographic information system (GIS)

A system of computer hardware, software, data, and workflow procedures for collecting, storing, analyzing and disseminating information about areas of the earth. People interact with a GIS to integrate, analyze, and visualize geographic data; identify relationships, patterns, and trends; and help find solutions to problems. Each GIS typically represents map information as data layers used to perform analysis and visualization.

geometry

The measures and properties of points, lines, polygons, surfaces, and 3D objects. In a GIS, geometry is used to represent the spatial component of geographic features. There are two primary geometry types: features and rasters (often called grids).

geoprocessing

The methodical execution of a sequence of operations on geographic data to create new information. Common geoprocessing operations are geographic feature overlay, feature selection and analysis, topology processing, raster processing, and data conversion. Geoprocessing allows you to chain together sequences of tools, feeding the output of one tool into another. You can use this ability to compose a variety of geoprocessing models (tool sequences) that help automate your work, perform analysis, and solve complex problems.

georeferencing

The process of describing the correct location and shape of features—typically by assigning coordinates from a known reference system, such as latitude/longitude, universal transverse mercator (UTM), or State Plane. Georeferencing allows various independent GIS datasets to be brought together as overlays of geographic information.

GIS

See geographic information system (GIS).

Global Positioning System (GPS)

A system of satellites and receiving devices used to compute positions on the earth for three dimensions (x, y, and z). GPS is used in navigation, mapping, GIS, and surveying.

grid

See raster.

image

A raster-based representation or description of a scene, typically produced by an optical or electronic device, such as a camera or a scanning radiometer. Common examples include remotely sensed data (for example, satellite imagery), scanned data, and photographs.

image catalog

See raster catalog.

key

See primary key.

layer

In ArcGIS, a reference to a data source, such as a geodatabase feature class, raster, shapefile, and so on, that defines how the data should be symbolized on a map or in a 3D document such as in ArcGlobe. Layers can also define additional properties, such as which features from the data source are included. Layers can be stored in map documents (.mxd) or saved individually as layer files (.lyr).

line

A shape having length and direction but no area, connecting at least two x,y coordinates. Lines represent geographic features too narrow to be displayed as an area at a given scale, such as contours, street centerlines, or streams, or features with no area that form the boundaries of polygons, such as state and county boundary lines.

line feature

In ArcGIS, a digital representation of a place or thing that has length but is too narrow to be represented as a polygon area at a particular scale, such as a river on a world map or a street on a city map.

map

1. A graphic depiction on a flat surface of the physical features of the whole or a part of the earth or other body, using shapes to represent objects and symbols and labels to represent the feature properties or descriptions. Maps generally use a specified projection and indicate the direction of orientation.

2. A collection of map elements laid out and organized on a page. Common map elements include the map frame with map layers, a scale bar, north arrow, title, descriptive text, and a symbol legend. The primary map element is the map frame, which provides the principal display of geographic information. Within the map frame, geographical entities are presented as a series of map layers that cover a given map extent—for example, map layers such as roads, rivers, place names, buildings, political boundaries, surface elevation, and satellite imagery.

3. The document used in ArcMap to display and work with geographic data. In ArcMap, a map contains one or more layers of geographic data, contained in data frames, and various supporting map elements, such as a scale bar. Often referred to as an "ArcMap document" or an "MXD."

metadata

Information that describes the content, quality, condition, origin, and other characteristics of a dataset or other pieces of information. Metadata consists of properties and documentation. Properties are derived from the data source (for example, the coordinate system and projection of the data), while documentation is entered by a person (for example, keywords used to describe the data).

model

1. An abstraction and description of reality used to represent objects, processes, or events.

2. In ArcGIS, a geoprocessing model that implements a clearly defined procedure created using the MobleBuilder application or written as a Python script. Geoprocessing is used to chain together sequences of tools, feeding the output of one tool into another. Geoprocessing models are used to derive new information from input data.

3. In the geodatabase, the schema of any particular geodatabase instance. In this case, the data model describes the objects that are represented in the geodatabase, their rules and GIS behaviors, and their relationships to each other.

4. A data representation of reality, such as the vector data model, raster data model, or relational data model.

ModelBuilder

A geoprocessing application in ArcGIS used with ArcToolbox to graphically compose a geoprocessing model or script.

multipatch

1. A type of geometry used to represent the outer surface, or shell, of features that occupy a discrete area or volume in three-dimensional space. They are comprised of planar 3D rings and triangles that are used in combination to model a feature.

2. A type of 3D feature class in the geodatabase.

multiuser geodatabase

A geodatabase managed in an RDBMS server by ArcSDE that supports transactions and versioning. Multiuser geodatabases can be very large and support multiple, concurrent editors. They are supported on a variety of commercial RDBMSs including Oracle, Microsoft SQL Server, IBM DB2, and Informix. Often referred to as an ArcSDE geodatabase.

network

A set of connected edges, junctions, and other elements (such as complex turns in a transportation system), along with connectivity rules, that are used to represent and model the behavior of a common network infrastructure in the real world—for example, an interconnected set of lines representing a city streets layer, a pipeline, a sewer, or an electrical network.

Oracle

A leading RDBMS software product developed and owned by Oracle Corporation. It provides excellent client/server access to very large data collections and is used by many ArcGIS users for managing their geodatabases.

personal geodatabase

A geodatabase that stores data in a single-user Microsoft Access data file. A personal geodatabase can be read simultaneously by several users, but only one user at a time can write data into it.

point feature

In ESRI software, a digital representation of a place or thing that has location but is too small to have area or length at a particular scale, such as a city on a world map or a building on a city map. A point feature may also be used to represent a place or thing that by its nature doesn't have area or length, such as a mountain peak or the location of a lightning strike.

polygon feature

In ESRI software, a digital representation of a place or thing that has area at a particular scale, such as a country on a world map or a land parcel on a parcel map. Polygon features have polygon geometry and can be singlepart or multipart. For example, the state of Hawaii can be represented using a series of polygons for its many islands.

primary key

A column or set of columns in a database that uniquely identifies each record. A primary key allows no duplicate values and cannot be NULL.

query

A request that selects features or records from a database. A query is often written as a statement or logical expression.

raster

A spatial data model that defines space as an array of equally sized cells arranged in rows and columns. Each cell contains an attribute value and location coordinates. An image uses a rater data structure.

raster catalog

A collection of raster datasets defined in a table of any format, in which the records define the individual raster datasets that are included in the catalog. A raster catalog is used to display adjacent or overlapping raster datasets without having to mosaic them together into one large file.

RDBMS

Relational database management system. A type of database in which the data is organized across several tables. Tables are associated with each other through common fields. Data items can be recombined from different files. Structured Query Language (SQL) is a language for working with the rows, columns, and data types in an RDBMS.

relational database management system (RDBMS)

See RDBMS.

shapefile

A vector data storage format, invented and published by ESRI for storing the location, shape, and attributes of geographic features. A shapefile is stored in a set of related files and contains one feature class. Shapefiles are widely used for data interchange among heterogeneous GIS systems.

SOAP

Simple Object Access Protocol. An XML-based protocol developed by Microsoft, Lotus, and IBM for exchanging information between peers in a decentralized, distributed environment. SOAP allows programs on different computers to communicate independently of operating system or platform by using the World Wide Web's HTTP and XML as the basis of information exchange. SOAP is now a W3C specification.

SQL

See Structured Query Language (SQL).

Structured Query Language (SQL)

A syntax for defining and manipulating data from a relational database. Developed by IBM in the 1970s, SQL has become an industry standard for query languages in most relational database management systems.

table

A set of data elements arranged in rows and columns. Each row represents an individual entity, record, or feature, and each column represents a single field or attribute value. A table has a specified number of columns but can have any number of rows.

tool

A geoprocessing operator in ArcGIS that performs specific geoprocessing tasks such as clip, split, erase, or buffer. A tool can belong to any number of toolsets and/or toolboxes. ArcToolbox organizes all the geoprocessing tools in ArcGIS in separate toolboxes and toolsets.

topology

In geodatabases, the arrangement that constrains how point, line, and polygon features share geometry. For example, street centerlines and census blocks share geometry, and adjacent soil polygons share geometry. Topology defines and enforces data integrity rules (for example, there should be no gaps between polygons). It supports topological relationship queries and navigation (for example, navigating feature adjacency or connectivity), supports sophisticated editing tools, and allows feature construction from unstructured geometry (for example, constructing polygons from lines).

transaction

1. A group of data operations that comprise a complete operational task, such as inserting a row into a table.

2. A logical unit of work as defined by a user. Transactions can be data definition (create an object), data manipulation (update an object), or data read (select from an object).

vector

A coordinate-based data model that represents geographic features as points, lines, and polygons. Each point feature is represented as a single coordinate pair, while line and polygon features are represented as ordered lists of vertices. Attributes are associated with each feature.

version

In geodatabases, a snapshot in time of the state of a geodatabase used to manage many key GIS data management workflows. These workflows include:

- Multiuser editing where each user is editing his or her own version.

- Checkout, disconnect, edit, and check updates back in.

- Creating historical archives.

- Synchronizing updates across a series of distributed geodatabase replicas.

XML

See eXtensible Markup Language (XML).